SEMINAR STUDIES IN HISTORY

Early Tudor Parliaments
1485–1558

SEMINAR STUDIES IN HISTORY

General Editor: Roger Lockyer

Early Tudor Parliaments 1485–1558

Michael A. R. Graves

Associate Professor of History
University of Auckland, New Zealand

LONGMAN
London and New York

Longman Group UK Limited,
Longman House, Burnt Mill, Harlow,
Essex CM20 2JE, England
and Associated Companies thoughout the world.

Published in the United States of America
by Longman Inc., New York

First Published 1990

Set in 10/11 point Baskerville (Linotron)
Printed in Malaysia
by Sun U Book Co. Sdn. Bhd., Petaling Jaya, Selangor Darul Ehsan

ISBN 0 582 03497 3

British Library Cataloguing in Publication Data
Graves, Michael A. R.
Early Tudor parliaments, 1485–1558. – (Seminar studies in
history)
I. Title   II. Series
328.4109

ISBN 0–582–03497–3

Library of Congress Cataloging in Publication Data
Graves, Michael A. R.
Early Tudor parliaments, 1485–1558/Michael A. R. Graves.
p.   cm. – (Seminar studies in history)
Includes bibliographical references (p.   ).
ISBN 0–582–03497–3: £3.75
1. Great Britain. Parliament – History.   2. Great Britain –
Politics and government – 1485–1603.   I. Title.   II. Series.
JN521.G724   1990   89–13893
328.42'09 – dc20   CIP

Cover: Illustration from Procession Roll for the Parliament of 1512,
showing King Henry VIII walking in procession beneath a canopy.
Master and Fellows of Trinity College Cambridge.

Contents

Contents

Seminar Studies in History
Founding Editor: Patrick Richardson

Introduction

The Seminar Studies series was conceived by Patrick Richardson, whose experience of teaching history persuaded him of the need for something more substantial than a textbook chapter but less formidable than the specialised full-length academic work. He was also convinced that such studies, although limited in length, should provide an up-to-date and authoritative introduction to the topic under discussion as well as a selection of relevant documents and a comprehensive bibliography.

Patrick Richardson died in 1979, but by that time the Seminar Studies series was firmly established, and it continues to fulfil the role he intended for it. This book, like others in the series, is therefore a living tribute to a gifted and original teacher.

Note of the System of References:
A bold number in round brackets (**5**) in the text refers the reader to the corresponding entry in the Bibliography section at the end of the book. A bold number in square brackets, preceded by 'doc.' [**doc. 6**] refers the reader to the corresponding item in the section of Documents, which follows the main text. A word followed by an asterisk indicates that the term is defined in the glossary.

ROGER LOCKYER
General Editor

Part One: The Background

1 Medieval Origins to 1399

Co-operation and consent

Medieval English kings, like their counterparts on the Continent, were accustomed to consult the great men of the land on matters of common concern. It was political commonsense to do so in the interest of both political stability and royal authority. These Great Councils, in which the King conferred with the nobles and bishops, were meetings between a feudal overlord and his vassals. He summoned them individually to assist him; they owed him a personal obligation; and they had no sense of common purpose or of responsibility to a wider community. The parliaments which emerged from the Great Councils, however, were characterised by very different attitudes and membership. The great feudatories came to see themselves as spokesmen and sometimes even protectors of the kingdom against harsh, arbitrary or unjust royal government–or misgovernment. Furthermore they were joined by representatives of other important social orders and legal corporations, especially the cities and towns and (in England) the sub-noble rural class of gentry.

These were European developments but, even as parliaments appeared, their experiences diverged. Continental assemblies closely mirrored the way in which society was structured in orders or estates. So the French Estates-General and the *Cortes* of Spain had separate chambers for the clergy, nobility, and the third estate (which encompassed the rest of society, although in practice, its membership was usually restricted to representatives of the towns). In contrast, at no time did English parliaments conform to the Continental model (**97**, p. 38). Furthermore, whilst most European assemblies were the product of royal initiative and patronage, it might be argued that in England they were, in origin, an expedient weapon of resistance and a restraint on royal power. Thus in 1264-5 the baronial opposition to Henry III sought a wider basis of support, when it treated with representatives from towns and counties about urgent reforms. However, Henry's son and successor, Edward I (1272–1307), was quick to see and utilise the benefits of such occasions. Thereafter parliaments were fostered and nurtured by a succession of kings. They provided an opportunity to govern with the co-operation and financial assistance of power groups which extended beyond the old feudal circle of noble and ecclesiastical vassals. This co-operative principle strengthened royal government, but, at the same time, it placed restraints on royal authority. For example, by 1377, when Edward III died, it had been firmly established that no new law could be made, and no tax levied, without parliamentary consent.

The monarchy did not relinquish ultimate control of Parliament as it developed. The King alone decided when it should meet, how often, and for how long. Moreover, he determined both its membership and the matters to be discussed. Nevertheless, unlike the earlier Great Councils, parliaments embodied the concept of the community's consent: that what concerned everyone should be approved by everyone. Certainly the overwhelming majority of people did not participate in the choice of Parliament's membership and so were not directly represented. But in the fourteenth century contemporaries referred to the 'whole realm in Parliament' and described the institution as the 'community of the realm'. Politically astute kings might exploit co-operation and consent in Parliament to their own advantage, but ineffectual or inept rulers, such as Edward II (1307–27) and Richard II (1377–99), did not, and they suffered the penalties of political failure and deposition as a consequence. On the other hand, the medieval assemblies did not acquire the power to depose monarchs. That was a constitutional impossibility, because the King alone could call a legitimate Parliament into being. On both occasions the business of deposition was performed by a meeting of the *estates* of Parliament, together with London citizens and others representing the *populus*. Nevertheless such special assemblies and ordinary parliaments had one common characteristic: they were recognised as representative of the community of all the realm, a far cry from the narrow, unrepresentative nature of Parliament's ancestor, the Great Council.

In contrast, there was no significant difference between the functions of those early medieval gatherings (known as Great Councils because they were meetings of the King's Council, enlarged by the presence of summoned bishops and nobles) and the emerging parliaments. The former met to give counsel to the King – rather than to make decisions – on a wide range of matters such as taxation, administration, the political situation and, in particular, judgements to be delivered by his Court. The consultative process and the provision of justice were also essential features of the early parliaments. Whilst, for example, the resolution of 'great affairs' was foremost in Edward I's mind when he summoned an assembly, there was also a popular expectation that it was an occasion on which justice might be sought and received from the King or his Council. This was reflected in the use of the term 'High Court of Parliament'. It was also given practical expression in the hearing of pleas and the many petitions handed in for consideration each time Parliament met. This was especially true in the first century of its recognisable existence after the political conflict between Henry III and a baronial opposition (1258–65).

During the same period, however, the functions of Parliament underwent significant change and, in the process, became more clearly defined. Its consent to taxes and new laws became binding on the crown. Common petitions, which touched the community-at-large, were increasingly remedied by legislative instead of judicial process. Private bills embodying the grievances of private persons and interests (or the injustices supposedly done to them), were delivered to receivers and triers who forwarded them to a government department or law court for a solution. And although consultation on 'great affairs' remained a vital function of Parliament, its deliberations frequently resulted in the enactment of new laws.

The emergence of the House of Commons

Parliamentary developments during the fourteenth century, especially in Edward III's reign (1327–77), radically altered the structure of the institution. At some point, and certainly by 1332, the knights and burgesses began to deliberate together and apart from their social betters, the archbishops, bishops, abbots and nobles. Despite this separation, Parliament remained the exception to the estate-structure of most European assemblies. The great ecclesiastics (the lords spiritual) and the nobles (the lords temporal) continued to sit together in the original Parliament house, instead of dividing into their own estates and occupying separate venues. Furthermore the King's professional counsel – his judges, Attorney, Solicitor, and serjeants – which, along with the rest of his Council, had always formed the nucleus of Parliament, remained with them in what would become known in the sixteenth century as the House of Lords.

The new lower, 'nether', or Commons' House of knights and burgesses had a significant impact on the development of fourteenth-century parliaments. Its right to initiate direct taxes was firmly

established and it quickly learned to relate redress of grievances to
financial grants. Although, unlike the Lords, its members were not
summoned to advise and treat, but simply to consent, they displayed
a capacity to initiate political debate, criticise royal administration,
and join with members of the other House in opposition to the King,
especially Richard II. Nor did they always follow unquestioningly
the political lead of the nobility. And as Parliament acquired the
sole and prescriptive right to make new laws, the Commons' participation in the process grew in importance. This was primarily
because of its representative nature. The burgesses in particular
were frequently charged with the responsibility to protect, confirm,
or enlarge the liberties of their cities and towns and to promote their
petitions. As many of these latter sought the redress of local grievances, members acted individually as custodians of local interests.
They also became, collectively, the guardians of the wider interests
of the community, criticising administrative corruption, or the
King's failure to consult, and even attacking unpopular royal ministers and favourites. It was in the furtherance of this role that the
Commons worked with the Lords to develop the impeachment procedure: the former laid charges against a particular individual and
the latter sat in judgement on him. In this way prominent servants
and friends of Edward III and Richard II were punished; and in
the process Parliament asserted the principle of ministerial responsibility to the community as well as to the King.

The extent and nature of change in fourteenth-century parliaments should not be exaggerated or misunderstood. There was no
growing assault on royal authority. Impeachment, for example, was
simply a parliamentary response to particular crises or inept
monarchs. Furthermore, the thirteenth-and fourteenth-century
crises which resulted in impeachments, baronial uprisings and
royal depositions were the exception, not the rule. Medieval kings
and the community sought consensus and agreement, and cooperation tended to be the norm in monarch–Parliament relations.
Within Parliament itself the Commons was unquestionably inferior.
The Upper House had more developed procedures, and enjoyed
the assistance of the King's legal counsel. Its members, possessed
of great social and political power and prestige, could influence the
election of Commons' members in some constituencies. In contrast
the organisation of the Lower House was at an early stage: its first
recorded Speaker was chosen as late as 1376. Above all, its law-
making role remained subordinate to that of the King and Upper
House. It was not yet one of the three assenting parties to new laws,

but a petitioner which received vague and general responses to its loosely-worded supplications.

The membership of parliaments

The King continued to be far more important than either Lords or Commons. It was he who commanded all members to come with full authority to bind those whom they represented to whatever was decided. He also determined the life and composition of parliaments. That composition had changed considerably since the early days when the King and his Council had met with the clergy and baronage, briefly afforced by the presence of knights and burgesses. Before 1400 the King's Council had ceased to sit as a body apart from the professional counsel in the Lords; and the lower clergy disappeared, attending instead the Convocations (provincial assemblies) of the Church. Such changes were dependent on the royal will. So was the calling of lords spiritual and temporal to the early parliaments and to the Upper House which emerged in Edward III's reign. Normally the two archbishops and nineteen bishops were all expected to attend, and some twenty to thirty abbots. The number of nobles attending fluctuated: some were minors and thus ineligible and others were serving the crown in a military capacity elsewhere. In any case, the King alone decided who to summon, and whether to summon them regularly, sometimes, or not at all. Those who owed a personal obligation to him and whose counsel he desired could be commanded to render parliamentary service. Time, custom and usage were to reduce his initiative.

Likewise it was the King's decision whether or not to afforce parliamentary meetings with representatives of the counties (knights of the shire) and boroughs (burgesses). Frequently they were not called to the early parliaments: however, when the institution divided into two Houses, with the Commons as petitioner and the King and Lords as judges, their presence became essential to the work of the 'High Court of Parliament'. Nevertheless it was still the monarch who directed that knights and burgesses should be elected. Moreover, whilst he usually required the return of knights from each county, his government was freely discriminating about borough membership. In the thirteenth century, especially, the cities and towns which were represented fluctuated between about a score and more than a hundred. Gradually, however, the variations diminished. Some urban communities, especially London, regularly elected members to fourteenth-century parliaments. Others remained unrepresented or were dropped off the list of parliamentary boroughs. But the parliamentary enfranchisement of boroughs remained in the crown's gift, as the Tudors' many additions were to demonstrate.

The place of parliaments

By 1399 parliaments had become a political focal point of the kingdom whenever they met, whether in co-operative mood or in crisis. From the mid-thirteenth century they had met frequently, often annually and even more than once a year – a fact which must have contributed to the growth of parliamentary traditions and practices. Inevitably the Commons, as the newcomer, lagged behind the Lords. It did not acquire its own Clerk and Speaker until Edward III's reign, whereas the Upper House inherited the services of the Chancery clerks and the King's professional counsel from the earlier unicameral Parliament. Unlike the more ordered, organised Lords, its conduct of affairs was haphazard and the product of chance rather than of design. In any case, despite the deposition of two kings (in 1327 and 1399), in normal times the monarch remained the most potent force in these meetings with the community. The parliaments were, after all, only brought into brief existence when he needed counsel and assistance. Against this must be balanced the way in which baronial oppositions had learned to use parliaments to resist and to reform. And the Commons' members, especially the knights of the shire, were capable of spirited criticism and action in cooperation with, or even despite, the Lords. The conduct of parliaments, whether collaborative or confrontational, had advanced their importance and diminished royal potency during their sessions. That process was to continue in the fifteenth century.

2 Lancaster and York, 1399-1485

The political context

The important political developments in the fifteenth century were, to a large extent, the consequences of the dual legacy of Edward III. One was the brood of sons which he sired. He endowed them with estates and the Dukedoms of Clarence, Lancaster and York. They in turn founded noble dynasties which, by marriages, extended their kinship connections through a large part of the English nobility. Therefore future kings had to heed the interests of a group of powerful, ambitious families, each one connected by blood to the royal line. Not that any of them schemed to displace Edward III's grandson and heir, Richard II. If he provided 'good governance' and did not alienate them by patently unjust actions, there was little prospect of ambitions reaching so high. However, Richard failed on both counts. In 1399 he was deposed and the vacant throne was occupied by another of Edward's grandsons, Henry of Lancaster.

Henry IV's usurpation highlighted a constitutional weakness which plagued England for most of the fifteenth century. There were no precise rules governing the descent of the crown, apart from the general principle of heredity within the ruling family (**34**, pp. 76–8). This imprecision worked to Henry's advantage in 1399, but thereafter it bedevilled the Lancastrian dynasty. After all, the new King was one of the magnates. And some of them (such as York) could present legitimate claims to sit in the place of a usurper, whose right by descent was open to question. The only way in which Henry IV (1399–1413) and his successors could justify occupancy of the throne was by the provision of good government.

In the reign of his son, Henry V (1413–22), however, the second of Edward III's legacies returned to haunt the Lancastrians: the revival of his claim to the French crown and the resumption of military campaigns in France. Successful foreign war was politic, because it diverted abroad the energies and attention of the nobility. It was also popular because it was profitable and prestigious. Under Henry V's leadership it was certainly successful, yielding profit, conquests and the promise of the French crown. However, Lancaster was now committed to an adventurous, expensive foreign policy. If success turned to failure, disillusionment and opposition to the dynasty were likely to follow. Henry VI (1422–61) was only an infant when he succeeded his father. There followed, in consequence, a long period of regency government in which great nobles dominated the King's Council and Parliament. Their governance was characterised by division and conflict. Nor did the situation change significantly when Henry came of age in 1437. He was meek, gentle, saintly, subject to bouts of mental illness, and ill-equipped to govern. As public disorder and lawlessness spread, the conviction grew that he was unfit to rule, and the House of York moved from the wings on to the stage, as a contender for the crown. Another calamity for Henry VI was the loss of the French 'empire' – by 1453 only Calais remained in English hands. Lancaster had failed to secure France or provide good governance at home. The discredited Lancastrians drifted into intermittent civil war with the Yorkists, and in 1461 Henry was deposed.

The new Yorkist usurper Edward IV (I461–83) proved himself able to provide the effective government which the Lancastrians had not, despite threats to his security and the brief restoration of Henry VI in 1470–1. The events of 1483–5, when his brother Richard usurped the throne of his son, Edward V, marked the end of the Yorkist regime, because Richard III was defeated and killed by yet another claimant, Henry Tudor. However, this was just a brief interlude in the recovery of royal government started by the Yorkists and continued by the victorious Lancastrian Henry VII.

Institutional developments

Parliament underwent further change and development in the fifteenth century. It remained first and foremost, as it always had been, 'the High Court of Parliament' and both judges and theorists repeatedly emphasised its 'curial' quality. Yet, at the same time, it was generally recognised as the political venue in which the nation's great affairs were treated and resolved. Moreover the practical importance of this political function gradually superseded that of its judicial activity. This was because Parliament increasingly provided legislative solutions – new laws – rather than judicial ones for the problems and issues which came before it. Furthermore, one of its greatest judicial weapons, the trial of prominent men by impeachment, was not used again after 1450 until the early seventeenth century.

The growing practice of responding to both public needs and private grievances with new laws was closely related to another fifteenth-century parliamentary development: the way in which the institution acquired internal unity. The House of Commons was central to both of these processes. In 1399 it was still a petitioner for redress of grievances, with the King and Lords sitting in judgement. In other words, Parliament still conducted itself very much like a law court. However, this rapidly changed during the first thirty years of Lancastrian rule. It became normal practice for petitions to be handed into the Commons, before they were passed to the King and Lords. It was not unusual even for royal proposals, couched in petitionary form, to be placed there first for consideration. Thus the Commons came to participate regularly in the process of enacting such petitions into law. In this way the Lower House was elevated during the fifteenth century from a mere petitioner to a full partner in the law-making process, and co-equal with the House of Lords.

At the same time the petition was transformed into the parliamentary bill. The former was often vaguely worded. Even if it received the assent of the King and Lords, they (or, in practice, the royal judges) were still free to redraft it as a law – a process which might significantly modify or even negate the intention and objective of the petitioners. In the mid-fifteenth century the advent of the parliamentary bill, which incorporated the precise wording of the law to be enacted, prevented such cavalier treatment. Although each House could amend the text of a bill, the assent of both of them was necessary to it in its final form. Thus the Commons' legislative parity with the Lords was assured. In the same way the claim of the Lower House to be the sole initiator of lay taxation was confirmed and reinforced. In 1407 it successfully protested against what it saw as the Lords' encroachment on that right. On other occasions it proved to be difficult about the size of the tax demanded, or unwilling to vote one at all. It even attempted (albeit unsuccessfully) to make taxation dependent on the redress of grievances.

The Commons' upward path was neither smooth nor free of obstacles. Its assertions and claims were frequently rejected by the King, graciously but nevertheless firmly. Its parliamentary influence diminished during the long aristocratic domination of Henry VI's reign. And although its relations with the Yorkist kings were more harmonious, the new dynasty called parliaments less often (**44**, pp. 278–85). In any case the Commons' newly-acquired parliamentary importance was not a political 'rise'. It did not constitute the first step on a long road which led to the seventeenth-century civil war and revolution. It was rarely involved in 'great affairs'; its members had no clearly-defined privileges in law; and in their social status, political influence and patronage, the knights and burgesses were but pygmies alongside the aristocratic and ecclesiastical giants of the Upper House.

The Lords, with its legal assistants and senior parliamentary bureaucrats, was superior in prestige and more efficient. Its collective membership was close to the King, and deeply involved in 'great affairs'. Moreover its extensive patronage network included many of the knights and burgesses who sat in the Lower House and whose election had been determined or influenced by great nobles or bishops. In any case, over and above both Houses was the King. He remained Parliament's motivating force, the man who breathed life into it whenever he chose. Although he remained apart from it and not a part of it (King *and* Parliament, not King *in* Parliament), he presided over it. His judges were there to assist the Lords. His Councillors managed both Houses in his interest. The Lord Chancellor, first among royal servants, guided the Upper House, whilst, as the role of Commons' Speaker developed, the King assumed control of his selection. So in 1485 Parliament was still a royal institution, activated to serve royal interests. And, despite the occasional willingness of knights and burgesses to criticise royal government, or to join with noble opponents of the King, there was no challenge to the divinely-ordained authority of the monarchy. The fifteenth-century rise of the Commons was an institutional process, whereby it became fully integrated into Parliament and co-equal with the Lords in the parliamentary function of law-making. That was the situation when the first Tudor, Henry VII, became King.

Parliamentary records and procedures

Between Edward I's accession in 1272 and Richard II's deposition, almost 200 parliaments – more than one a year – were called, whilst more than fifty met between 1399 and 1485. Their frequency and the increasing importance of their functions testify to a vigorous institutional growth. And like any other healthy, burgeoning institution, Parliament spawned its own records. The oldest of these, the Parliament Roll, underwent changes which reflected its increasing legislative importance. Until Richard III's solitary Parliament in 1484 the Roll gave an account of proceedings, but thenceforth it was confined almost entirely to the Acts passed. The same assembly was also the first to be followed by the publication of a set of printed statutes. This heralded the print revolution. The first English operators of the printing press were quick to discern the potential market for printed statutes among lawyers and magistrates, bureaucrats and the wider community. This was a commentary on the importance of Parliament as the maker of statute, the highest form of law.

If Parliament had its record (the Roll), the House of Lords, which was the older chamber and embodied the original nucleus of the institution, had its own also. Once again, the fifteenth century was a time of change. By 1453 (and probably earlier) the officer known as the Clerk of the Parliaments, who served the Upper House, was keeping an attendance register and a record of the enactment of bills into law. In contrast the Commons' clerk did not list those present or absent. It would have been an impossible task with a much larger body of members, who sat anywhere 'as they came' and not in strict order of precedence. Moreover, so far as we can tell, he did not record the Commons' proceedings before 1547 (see p. 24).

The absence of a Commons' Journal, the mere fragments of the Lords' record which survive, and the less and less informative Parliament Roll make it virtually impossible to comment meaningfully on the way in which the two Houses handled the legislative business before them. However, something can be gleaned from the surviving fragments of the fifteenth-century Lords' Journal, together with the Commons' diary kept by the burgesses who represented Colchester in the first Tudor parliament in 1485 (**26**). The two Houses were developing techniques for the efficient enactment of bills into statutes. However, it was the Lords, with its longer history, more experienced membership, and assistance from the judges, which pioneered innovations and led the way.

Membership and attendance

In the fifteenth century the composition and size of the House of Commons became fixed: seventy-four knights of the shire and, despite earlier fluctuations, 222 burgesses (borough members). Parliament also regularised elections to its lower chamber. A statute of 1406 ordained that all freemen who were present at the county court could vote for the shire members in a free and impartial election.

And another, in 1413, imposed a residential qualification on parliamentary burgesses. Thereafter, however, various socio-political forces altered or undermined the terms of these Acts. Parliament's growing importance transformed membership from a duty into a desirable privilege. Aristocratic dominance in Henry VI's reign and faction conflict in the fifteenth-century dynastic wars extended to interference in elections. Members of the emerging class of gentry sought seats in their own interest. The cumulative effect of these forces was an increasing oligarchic control of the electoral process. Country gentlemen ignored the terms of the 1413 statute and 'invaded' the boroughs. As early as 1422 one-quarter of the parliamentary burgesses were non-residents. And, by the middle of the century, the hand of great magnates can be detected in borough elections.

Oligarchic control was strengthened by statutes which increasingly restricted the Commons' membership. In 1429 the exercise of the vote in county elections was limited to freeholders worth forty shillings a year, thereby disfranchising both lesser freeholders and landless freemen. Sixteen years later an Act of Parliament ruled that counties should be represented by men of 'the better sort': knights, esquires or substantial gentlemen. The foundations were laid for three centuries of parliamentary dominance by the 'landed interest'. Not that they enjoyed a monopoly: alongside the gentry sat wealthy merchants who represented the powerful economic elites of the more important cities, such as London, York, Bristol and Norwich. The tightening grip of rural and urban oligarchies on the Commons' membership was one of the major parliamentary developments of the fifteenth century. The Upper House, and the peers in particular, played a prominent part in the growth of this oligarchic control. Although the process was still in its early days, the kin, retainers, clients or fee'd* lawyers of magnates were already being returned.

The King was still the most important single influence on the membership of Parliament and its size. He alone could enlarge the Commons by the enfranchisement of boroughs. By creating peers or securing their attainder he varied the size of the nobility, and he still exercised a certain discretion in the issue or denial of writs of summons to the House of Lords. However, his freedom of action was narrowing as time and custom established the right of nobles to be called individually and made it the distinguishing mark of peerage. Furthermore the two archbishops and nineteen bishops were invariably instructed to attend, whilst the despatch of writs to some 'regulars' (abbots and priors) was also being standardised. Both the lords spiritual (clergy) and lords temporal (nobility) placed an increasing value on the receipt of an individual summons. And when they turned up, the nobles in particular expected to be given precedence according to the seniority and antiquity of their titles. The seating arrangements in the Lords' chamber, where everyone sat in his due place, reflected this concern. Nevertheless, members of the Upper House were often less than willing to shoulder the parliamentary responsibilities which went with their privileged position. The abbots were notorious absentees; it was not uncommon for half the bishops to stay away; and, although some of the dukes, earls and other great magnates were more diligent, the attendance record of the late medieval nobility was generally very poor. Such persistent and widespread backsliding resulted in the first recorded imposition of fines on defaulters in Henry VI's reign. The problem was a serious one. The Lords' membership, fluctuating between 80 and 100, was much smaller than that of the Commons, and endemic absenteeism could seriously impair its business efficiency. This laxity had another practical consequence: whilst the lords spiritual had a paper majority, it often disappeared because of the high incidence of absenteeism among the regulars – long before the Dissolution of the Monasteries in 1539–40 created a permanent lay majority (**42**).

The business and politics of parliaments

The changes which took place in the fifteenth century did not fundamentally alter Parliament, but rather built on what had gone before. It remained the King's institution. He summoned and ended it, presided over it, and frequently attended the Lords' meetings. Although the Commons was integrated into the legislative activity of the institution, it still remained outside Parliament proper. This was physically and visibly expressed at the opening and closing ceremonies, when its members could not proceed into the Parliament chamber beyond the bar (or rail) placed across the lower end of the House. Even after it had attained co-equal legislative authority with the Lords, the King was prepared to add provisos to Commons' bills which had passed both Houses. Nevertheless, it made significant practical advances in the fifteenth century, especially in its business role. Its right to initiate lay taxes was unquestioned; its petitions, now bills in the form of the final Act, ranged across personal, local and commonweal matters; and even the crown chose to place some of its proposals there first (see p. 9). Indeed, Parliament as a whole had become a legislative clearing-house for royal needs, public concerns, and private grievances. Statute encompassed a broad spectrum of human affairs: social and economic, judicial and political. Yet it was not omnicompetent. Matters spiritual and any general modification or suppression of property rights remained beyond its legitimate sphere of activity.

Parliaments also continued to be political occasions. However, this should not be equated with conflict. Parliamentary politics, especially under the Lancastrians, were sometimes characterised by disagreement, opposition to royal policies, and competition for power. In contrast were the assemblies which met during the popular reign of Henry V, the parliamentary torpor of much of Henry VI's reign (at least until the disastrous years of the 1450s), and the relative harmony of Edward IV's parliaments. It made little difference whether the country was in political crisis and turmoil or not. Whenever a parliament met, every interested party from the King downwards engaged in politics to achieve their various ends. At the highest level, Parliament's continuing purpose was to meet the crown's financial and other needs and to settle the great affairs of the realm. However, it was also an opportunity to make laws for the public good, satisfy the aspirations of the ambitious, benefit economic interests, and heal the wounds of the aggrieved. Whatever the end, the means was parliamentary politicking. Approaches to the Commons' Speaker, *douceurs** to men of influence, the canvassing of opinion, and lobbying for support during the passage of bills were becoming accustomed practices. This was no less true under the Yorkists than during the Lancastrian regime. Strong Yorkist monarchy put the royal house in order, and called only seven parliaments in twenty-four years. Nevertheless it was not a despotic 'New Monarchy' (see p. 15). It still needed parliaments for taxes and new laws, and men of all sorts and conditions continued to turn to these assemblies to resolve their problems and advance their interests. For all these reasons, the future of the institution of Parliament was assured, no matter how infrequently it was called in a particular reign.

Part Two: Analysis

3 The Place of Parliament under the Early Tudors

The political context

Four Tudor monarchs ruled England between 1485 and 1558. The first of these, Henry VII, founded a new royal dynasty when he defeated and killed Richard III at Bosworth Field. His military success brought Yorkist government to an end and marked the final victory of the Lancastrian cause. Furthermore, in the system of government by personal monarchy the advent of a new King was always accompanied by alterations in policy and the style of kingship. Such alterations were inevitable, reflecting as they did the different personalities and personal preferences of the man who wore the crown for the time being. However, this did not amount to a change in the *nature* of royal government. Contrary to the view which was propagated in the latter part of Queen Victoria's reign, and which was accepted well into this century, neither the Yorkists nor the first Tudor introduced a 'New Monarchy'. According to this thesis, the 'new monarchs' adopted novel techniques, recruited a new breed of middle-class administrators, and were more concerned to acquire power than to protect the subjects' liberties. In reality the Yorkists did no more than halt the decline of royal authority, which had come near to collapse during the dynastic wars of the fifteenth century. Henry VII simply carried on the work of the dynasty which he had displaced when he continued the process of restoring 'good governance'.

Like all his medieval predecessors, and the Tudor monarchs who were to follow him, Henry VII's government operated in an *ad hoc* manner, responding to changing circumstances and dealing with problems as they arose. Without a police force or standing army, ample treasury or independent power to tax or legislate, his freedom of action was strictly circumscribed. Although English kings enjoyed a certain discretionary authority outside the law, it behove them to use it discreetly and only occasionally. After all, the crown was dependent on a largely unpaid landed governing elite to administer the kingdom at its direction – and that was the group most likely to be harmed and alienated by royal actions of an arbitrary kind. In any case, Henry VII's position was vulnerable, especially in the early years of his reign. His hereditary claim to the crown was not strong. Yorkist supporters and pretenders remained a threat for many years; lawlessness was endemic; the crown was impoverished, and its control of many localities was tenuous, even non-existent. Henry VII's achievement was to secure the new dynasty with an admixture of hard work, undramatic attention to detail, firmness (even harshness), and acts of pacification. By the time of his death in 1509, he had diminished, even if he had not actually resolved, some of the most pressing problems which had beset England and the crown for much of the fifteenth century.

The first Tudor's successor epitomised the way in which a new reign could dramatically alter the style of kingship. Not only were they men of contrasting personality, they also came to the throne in very different circumstances. Henry VIII was the heir of his father's marriage to Elizabeth of York, a marriage designed both to pacify the two warring dynasties of the fifteenth century and to reinforce the Tudors' hereditary claims. Henry VII's role had been one of undramatic labour towards the goals of dynastic security, good governance and financial solvency. His Court was by no means unimpressive, but it was always ordered according to his means. Furthermore, his foreign policy, which was for the most part diplomatic and pacific, even isolationist, was tailored to his over-riding financial concerns. In contrast Henry VIII's natural self-confidence was enhanced by his security of tenure. The inspiration of his kingship derived from the chivalric, militaristic and artistic Court of the fifteenth-century Dukes of Burgundy. The influence of this model had two significant consequences. Firstly, Henry's flamboyant and extrovert personality was expressed through his own ostentatious, cultivated and very costly Court. Secondly, he embarked on an expansive and expensive foreign policy. With an inflated opinion of his own importance in European affairs, he attempted to exploit the conflict between the Valois kings of France and Habsburg rulers of Germany and Spain. And he did so in pursuit of fluctuating objectives: the imperial or French crowns, enclaves of French territory, marriage alliances with Europe's ruling dynasties, or just the glory of great martial feats. Henry's means were equally varied: he led or despatched expeditions to France, subsidised allies and hired mercenaries; he wove flimsy alliances, and in 1520 participated in that futile diplomatic extravaganza, the Field of Cloth of Gold*.

Bishop Fisher condemned this last exercise as a sheer waste of money 'for no lasting good' (**72**, pp. 94–5).

The same could be said of all of Henry VIII's grandiose military and diplomatic activities during the first twenty years of his reign. Then, in 1529, he suffered a double humiliation. Francis I of France, to whose side he had switched only four years before, made peace with Henry's erstwhile ally, the Habsburg Charles V, without consulting him. At the same time the papacy, of which the English King had been the defender and supporter for much of the previous twenty years, refused to annul his marriage to Catherine of Aragon. This was a much more serious rebuff. The security of the Tudor dynasty required an undisputed succession. In other words, the designated heir should have credentials which were unimpeachable and certainly superior to those of any pretender – the fifteenth-century civil wars were not a remote memory. Ideally the heir should have been male and legitimate. However, by the 1520s the union of Henry and Catherine had produced only one surviving child, their daughter Mary. The Queen was ageing and the King's anxiety about the future of the dynasty was growing. His passion for Anne Boleyn, one of the court ladies, merged personal desire and political concern in a formidable combination. In the complex and sometimes squalid proceedings by which Henry sought to resolve his problems, only the central issues need to be rehearsed here. If the King was to marry Anne, his first marriage would have to be terminated. A divorce would be unacceptable to his Catholic subjects, who would not recognise the legitimacy either of a second marriage or of its offspring. Only an annulment of his marriage to Catherine – a declaration of its invalidity – would suffice. But after much procrastination the Pope, who alone could grant it, refused to do so.

The immediate victim was Henry VIII's first great minister, Thomas Wolsey. Between 1509 and 1515 he had risen to become Cardinal, Archbishop of York and Lord Chancellor. Thereafter he managed Church and State, organised Henry's armies and conducted his diplomacy. However, he could not survive the reversals of 1529 and his fall was even more dramatic than his rise. Instead Henry, with the guiding assistance of his second great minister, Thomas Cromwell, secured his annulment through the Reformation Parliament (1529–36). The solution to the King's dilemma was ecclesiastical schism. Between 1532 and 1534 a break with Rome and the establishment of a national Catholic Church, with Henry as its supreme head, were enacted into law by an anti-papal, anti-clerical governing class in Parliament. The first, and amenable, archbishop of Henry's Church duly annulled his marriage to Catherine in May 1533, four months after the King had secretly married Anne. In this way Henry's matrimonial problems were resolved for the time being. More important, a jurisdictional revolution in the Church and in Church-State relations was carried through. There was also a massive transfer of property to the crown when the monasteries were dissolved (1536–40); and a dramatic advance in the State-building process, with the suppression of franchises (territorial 'liberties' in which the exercise of royal authority was strictly curtailed) and the extension of English county administration and parliamentary representation to Wales. By the end of the decade a sovereign national State had emerged. Henry VIII had acquired power and wealth unparalleled in the history of English kingship, together with the exercise of a personal, supposedly God-given supremacy over the Church.

However, political circumstances are subject to frequent, sometimes dramatic change, and political power is often a transient thing. The European Reformation, sparked by Martin Luther's* famous protest in Germany in 1517, had created divided societies. The subjects' automatic allegiance to the monarch, as God's anointed, was now qualified, even determined, by their religious position. They displayed an increasing willingness to disobey or resist heretical monarchs and even to approve of tyrannicide (the putting to death of 'ungodly princes'). Likewise monarchs, both Catholic and Protestant, persecuted those subjects who were not their co-religionists. In their case, persecution was motivated not only by religious conviction but also by the desire to suppress politically subversive movements. The European Reformation was characterised by mutual intolerance, dogmatism and ideological division, and England was not exempt from its influence. Lutheranism infiltrated it during the 1520s and 1530s. Henry, perhaps influenced by the reformist leanings of Cromwell and Archbishop Cranmer, remained equivocal towards heresy, until 1539–40. Then he adopted a firm conservative stand with the parliamentary enactment of six crucial articles of Catholic faith, and he sacrificed Cromwell to his Catholic rivals at Court. Even then, however, his persecution of heretics was inconsistent and desultory, and he left the government of his young son, Edward VI, in the hands of closet-Protestants. By then English Protestantism was being refreshed and reinforced by the more radical movements of Strassburg, Zurich and, above all, John Calvin's* Geneva. England had become permanently, often bitterly, divided along ideological lines.

This was not the only legacy of Henry VIII's reign. His renewed wars against France and Scotland during the 1540s consumed unprecedented sums in parliamentary taxation; the shortfall had to be made up by debasement of the coinage and the sale of royal assets, in particular ex-monastic property. By 1547 more than half the gains accruing to the crown from the Dissolution had been liquidated, and already its prospects of future financial independence from Parliament had virtually disappeared. The eleven years and two short reigns following Henry's death were a time of social disturbance, economic hardship, religious and political conflict, and a continued decline of royal authority and wealth from the pinnacle of the 1530s. Aristocratic government in the name of a minor, Edward VI (1547–53), followed by the rule of a woman, Mary I (1553–8), automatically made royal government weaker and more vulnerable. Furthermore, Edward's reign was characterised by aristocratic misgovernment and political in-fighting: first under Protector Somerset (1547–9) and then the Duke of Northumberland (1549–53). Mary's marriage to a Spanish Habsburg, Philip, and England's disastrous involvement in war against France (on his behalf), made her government increasingly unpopular. Finally, and most important of all, the sponsorship of Protestantism by Edward's governors – moderate under Somerset, more radical under Northumberland – admitted the ardent disciples and doctrines of Zwingli and Calvin into England. The Marian Catholic reaction, characterised by persecution rather than reform, resulted in the burning of almost 300 heretics. In the process, it created a consuming hatred of popery and Catholicism which was to last for centuries. When Mary died, England was a deeply divided society.

The historiography of early Tudor parliaments

The historiography of this period lacks the heat and thunder engendered by those who debate the early Stuart parliaments and the causes of the English civil war. Yet it is still rich in controversy, claim and counter-claim. Moreover, the early Tudor parliaments and those of James I and Charles I share a common characteristic. For a long time they were examined in relation to a perceived growth of the House of Commons and a rise in conflict which culminated in the revolution of the mid-seventeenth century. Historians studied Tudor parliamentary history, not in its own right, but in relation to that cataclysmic event. This was particularly true of Elizabeth I's reign, which Sir John Neale made his own in the 1940s and 1950s (**73, 74**). The early Tudor parliaments were treated in similar fashion, for example by Wallace Notestein (**113**, pp. 1–24) and A. F. Pollard (**77**). The prime concern of these 'orthodox' historians was the political rise of Parliament and, within it, of the Commons, at the expense of both the monarch and the House of Lords. If they did not specifically seek, or claim to find, the roots of Stuart conflict in the pre-Elizabethan assemblies, their political orientation did colour the picture of Parliament which they painted. Politics and political growth, not business and productivity, seemed to be both the essence and most important feature of sixteenth-century parliamentary history. Yet Parliament was an institution which carried through many far-reaching changes, and regularly voted additional funds and statutory tools of government, at the crown's request. And it deserves to be studied in terms of its importance within the sixteenth century, not merely with an eye to future conflict.

Such a change of approach began in the 1960s. Although J. S. Roskell's priorities were still political, he concluded that the Tudor parliaments were more acquiescent to royal authority than their medieval predecessors (**114**). In contrast, S. E. Lehmberg's study of Henry VIII's assemblies paid a novel attention both to business and to the House of Lords (**68, 69**). Above all, beginning in the 1960s, Sir Geoffrey Elton challenged – at first by implication, and later more explicitly – the received 'orthodox' version of parliamentary history. Focussing his attention at first on the Henrician parliaments, but later extending his scrutiny to those of Elizabeth, he demonstrated that they were usually effectively managed, co-operative, and productive (**56, 95, 96, 97**). Historians, Elton prominent amongst them, began to focus their attention on previously neglected aspects of the institution: its procedures, membership, bureaucracy, records, and especially the nature of its businesss (**60, 61, 94, 99, 100, 101**). Thus there emerged what is now described as 'revisionism'. It is not a school of historians, but a fresh way of looking at Parliament as a kind of legislative marketplace, and as a bicameral institution in which the Lords was as important and, so it now seems, more efficient than the Commons (**60**). It does not question that King-in-Parliament grew in constitutional authority (see pp. 26–7), but that is very different from arguing that the Commons acquired more political muscle, which it used to challenge royal authority. Revisionism has been much more active in redrawing the parliamentary contours of Elizabeth's reign, and it is much more controversial in the field of early Stuart studies. Nevertheless it has also contributed to a reassessment of the early Tudor parliaments.

One consequence of the revisionist approach has been another look at the direction in which Parliament was heading between 1485 and 1529, and most particularly under Henry VII. Was it stagnating, or even declining in importance? Affirmative answers to these questions were the by-products of the thesis first publicly formulated by the historian J. R. Green in 1874. He described the Yorkists and the first Tudor as innovative architects of a 'New Monarchy' (see pp. 15–16), which was more efficient, autocratic and restrictive of freedom (**38**, pp. 97–104). Although the emergence of such a novel kind of kingship has been discredited, it was widely accepted for a long time. This in turn influenced historians' conception of Parliament as a static institution, subordinated and exploited by Henry VII, who called it only once in his last twelve years. In 1972 S. B. Chrimes wrote, in dismissive vein, that 'little or nothing of much significance occurred in the history of Parliament' during Henry's reign (**49**, p. 135). J. R. Lander went further and painted a gloomy picture of the declining importance of its taxing and law-making services under a King who had little love for it and was abetted by apathetic nobles and a compliant Lower House (**37**, pp. 62–3). But despite its near-quiescence, and its few meetings, Parliament's two vital functions of lay taxation and the enactment of statute, the highest form of law, guaranteed its future. Henry VIII's wars produced a flurry of parliaments. And after another lean period (1515–29), in which only one was called, he turned to it for a statutory solution to his marital problems (**61**, pp. 51–3).

This brings us, logically and chronologically, to a much more important and heated historiographical debate. Commencing in the 1950s G. R. Elton presented a new and provocative interpretation of the years 1529–40 and their significance. According to Elton, it was the King's Secretary, Thomas Cromwell, who proposed schism as the way to achieve the annulment of Henry VIII's marriage. Cromwell was the draftsman who devised the necessary laws and the manager who steered them through Parliament. At the same time, his fertile and inventive mind conceived and drew up a legislative programme which transferred enormous ecclesiastical wealth to the crown and unified the realm, so that the King's writ ran everywhere. Cromwell, in Elton's opinion, restructured the royal Council and administration, and initiated State experiments in social and economic planning. If there was a 'New Monarchy', it was created in the 1530s and the changes amounted to a revolution (**52, 53, 55, 56, 91**). Furthermore, in the process of carrying through

21

these changes, King-in-Parliament was transformed into the sovereign body of an independent nation-State, and its statute law became omnicompetent. Elton's thesis did not go unchallenged and it has been modified in many respects since then. Further research, some undertaken by his own students, has demonstrated significant threads of continuity with late medieval developments, the important contributions of others during Cromwell's supremacy, the *ad hoc* nature of some Cromwellian measures, and the continuation of administrative experiment and reform after his death in 1540. Much of this Elton himself has acknowledged. Yet the degree, nature, and impact of the changes (chiefly effected through Parliament) in the 1530s still warrant the label of 'revolution'. If Thomas Cromwell's originality of approach, initiative, and input were less than Elton at first thought, he nevertheless remains the most prominent and impressive royal servant in that revolutionary process – no matter how complex were its intellectual origins.

Elton's work also contributed to a revived interest in the parliaments of the two succeeding reigns (**60, 61, 65, 66, 67, 70, 71, 108**). Some of the studies were revisionist in nature. They rehabilitated the Upper House and gave due attention to parliamentary business as well as politics (**60, 103**). There is a danger, however, that, whilst revisionism has been a healthy corrective to the political orientation and Commons-fixation of the 'orthodox' interpretation, it may lead historians into error of another kind. Its concentration on the legislative function of Parliament has revealed the importance of that body to private interests, and the time and energy devoted to the expedition of their business. In 1986, however, J. Loach implicitly questioned one of the revisionist premises: that, because Parliament was recognised as an occasion to secure statutory benefits for the King's subjects, collectively or individually, the pressure to enfranchise boroughs came from the localities. Loach demonstrated that, on the contrary, the Commons' increasing size in the 1530s was due to the crown's initiative in creating safe seats for Councillors and other royal servants (**109**, pp. 117–34). This underlines the point that Henry was acutely aware, even if revisionists are less so, that parliaments which were called upon to deal with his 'urgent causes' and 'great affairs' might give rise to disagreement, conflict, and opposition. It was advisable to be well-prepared.

Among the most important of recent studies is the Neale Memorial Lecture delivered by Professor Patrick Collinson in 1987. Although this was specifically concerned with Elizabethan parliaments, it contained an important message for students of early

Tudor assemblies too. 'Sir Geoffrey Elton and Professor Graves', said Collinson, 'have moved [the furniture] about the room and have removed some of the fancier pieces, replacing them with plainer, more utilitarian articles. Many of the new arrangements are acceptable and represent a great improvement. But some of the original and ornate items of furniture deserve to be dusted down and restored to positions of honour.' In other words, in shedding much light on the workings and business of Parliament, revisionism has rendered a signal service. But in its extreme form, it tends to belittle, even deny, the existence of great and controversial issues. In this, Collinson is undoubtedly right. Revisionism has enabled us to assess contentious matters of high politics and principle in the overall context of parliamentary activity – to see them in their right perspective. However, it is now time to put those conflicts of principle and policy back into the history of parliaments. To quote Collinson again: 'I hope that it is not yet the case that historians of these Parliaments are to be subject to the same sort of inhibitions as those assemblies themselves, forbidden to mention great things but only permitted to speak of the shipping of fish' (**87**).

The records of Parliament

The records of Parliament reveal not only what the institution did, and how it did it, its business and procedures. They are also an historical commentary on the development of its bureaucracy and even on changes in its authority, importance and functions. Until the later fifteenth century the senior bureaucrat, the Clerk of the Parliaments, who attended the House of Lords in particular, but also served Parliament in general, was a Chancery official. Chancery was the oldest department of State. It was also the activating force, which issued writs for elections to the Commons and despatched individual summonses to bishops, abbots and nobles to attend the House of Lords. Its presiding officer, the Lord Chancellor, guided the affairs of the Upper House, and it was also the repository of Parliament's records. Therefore it was natural that the officials who served as scribes in the two Houses, and who acted as custodians of the laws which it enacted, should have been recruited from the Lord Chancellor's department. However, between the mid-fifteenth and sixteenth centuries significant changes occurred in the organisation of Parliament's secretariat, the scope and content of its records and the manner of their preservation.

First, the Clerk of the Parliaments gradually disengaged himself from his earlier Chancery attachment and set up an embryonic Parliament Office. From 1497, midway through Henry VII's reign, he retained the original manuscript Acts of Parliament, instead of transferring them to Chancery as he had formerly done. Indeed it is symbolic of this 'divorce' that John Taylor, the new Clerk in Henry VIII's first Parliament in 1510, had no experience of Chancery (**94**, p. 84). Taylor was also the legatee of other changes which had occurred before his appointment. Until 1484 the Parliament Roll had been the master record of the medieval institution, but then it changed from an account of proceedings to mere enrolment of the laws enacted (**99**, p. 97). Its redundancy as a record of proceedings may have been the consequence of a fifteenth-century innovation: by 1453, and possibly earlier, the Clerk was keeping a separate record of the Lords' attendance and its bill proceedings. For a long time, it was no more than a collection of worksheets, which he compiled to assist him in the performance of his parliamentary duties and which were not designed to be preserved. By 1515, however, the Clerk was compiling a permanent record which, in the second half of the sixteenth century, became the official Journal of the House (**94**).

It is not surprising that the House of Lords, as the original nucleus of Parliament and served by the senior parliamentary bureaucrat, should have acquired its own record of business at an earlier date than that relative newcomer, the Commons. The first surviving Journal of the Lower House, kept by the underclerk, dates only from the first Parliament of Edward VI in 1547. One other change, reflective of Parliament's institutional development, warrants mention here, because it concerns the appearance of another class of records, and the role of the clerks in their production. Until 1484 manuscript copies of sessional statutes were available for purchase. This was already a reflection of Parliament's importance as the institution which made the supreme form of law. But in 1484 (the last pre-Tudor Parliament) they were printed – an early achievement of the new technology (see p. 11). By 1515, and regularly thereafter, a wider public was provided with cheaper, speedier, and easier access to the accurate text of new statutes – and the Clerks of the Parliament, with whom the original manuscript copies resided, must have been instrumental in making them available to the printers (**94**, pp. 92–100). These developments notwithstanding, historians of the early Tudor parliaments are poorly served with source materials. Apart from the record of the members for Colchester in 1485 [**docs**

3, 26] no parliamentary diaries were compiled or, if they were, have not survived. Contemporary observers and chroniclers, with a few exceptions such as Edward Halle (**12**), have little to say about parliamentary proceedings, whilst many ambassadorial reports are biased, inaccurate, and must be discounted. Serious lacunae diminish the value even of official records. The original manuscript Acts now surviving commence only in 1497; no official Commons' record exists prior to 1547; and no Lords' Journals survive for Henry VII's reign, for 1512, 1514, or 1523, for all but one session of the Reformation Parliament (1529–36), or for Mary's first assembly in 1553 (see introduction to Part Four, Documents).

Institutional developments

The parliaments which met between Henry VII's accession in 1485 and 1523 (the last assembly before the revolutionary Reformation Parliament of 1529–36) rounded off the later medieval institutional developments. In particular, the House of Commons' legislative parity with the Lords received judicial confirmation in 1489, when the judges declared that its assent, as well as that of the Lords, was required to enact a bill into law. In consequence the Upper House, once the nucleus of parliaments, became just one chamber in a bicameral institution. Perhaps as a result of its new status, the Commons' 'intercommunings' with the medieval Lords were replaced by more formal joint conferences (**56**, p. 250). And the Crown too displayed a new respect when, during Henry VII's reign, it ceased the cavalier practice of adding provisos to Commons' bills after they had passed the two Houses.

These were not, however, the only changes. In 1516 the judges dispelled any surviving notion that English parliaments, like Continental assemblies, were meetings of social estates when they ruled that the first estate of bishops and abbots did not have to be present in the Upper House when a bill was passed. Furthermore, the early sixteenth-century Parliament shed its earlier curial character. Contemporaries might still call it 'the High Court', but its early medieval function of resolving the law in difficult or important cases had been displaced by its taxative and law-making functions. So, as the Lords ceased to adjudicate on Commons' petitions, but instead became a co-equal legislative partner, the receivers and triers of petitions underwent a classic English process: their places were not abolished but simply fossilised. The most important change of all occurred in the King's relationship with Parliament. Medieval monarchs, standing above and apart from it, had called it to treat of urgent affairs which could not be resolved elsewhere (**44**, p. 278; **61**, p. 39). By 1529, however, the King had become part of the institution: King and Parliament had become King-in-Parliament.

If there was change between 1485 and 1529, there was also continuity. Parliaments remained royal occasions, summoned as and when the monarch saw fit, to serve the purposes of royal government. They therefore met frequently – five times – in the first ten years of Henry VII's reign, as he consolidated his position. But he called only two during his remaining fourteen years, simply because the need for them lessened. Indeed, on the second occasion, in 1504, he advised his subjects that he would not call another for a long time. This may have been a calculated public-relations exercise, bound to win a warm response because a new session usually meant another tax. In contrast, Henry VIII's military adventures reactivated parliaments in 1510–15 (**61**, pp. 41–2). Their utility guaranteed their continued existence. On the other hand, that utility was limited by the restraints on their competence: what they could do. It was generally accepted that they could touch neither matters spiritual, which were the Church's preserve [**doc. 1**], nor property rights, which were jealously guarded by the propertied class in the Lords and Commons.

The annulment crisis and break with Rome in the 1530s swept away these limitations. Any lingering remnants of the notion that Parliament as the 'High Court' declared what the law was, but did not make new law, were consigned to oblivion. Although the Act of Supremacy (1534) was simply a declaratory law, which acknowledged Henry's headship of the Church as God-given [**doc. 2**], the accompanying Acts which dismantled papal authority and transferred it to the crown constituted a massive incursion into the once-prohibited area of matters spiritual. The suppression of franchises (1536), the Acts dissolving the monasteries (1536 and 1539), and the Statute of Uses (which in 1536 restored to the King all his financial rights over property held by feudal tenures) amounted to a property revolution, and one which was enacted by Parliament [**docs. 2, 28**]. By 1540 King-in-Parliament had emerged as the sovereign legislator, and not the King alone. Parliament now incorporated the political nation: thus Henry VIII told it in 1542 that he and its members were 'knit together in one body politic'. Its laws were not only supreme but omnicompetent [**doc. 2**]. The Acts which carried through a Protestant Reformation in Edward VI's reign (1547–53), and then briefly restored Roman Catholicism under

Mary (1553–8), were made 'by authority of Parliament'. This was confirmation of the untrammelled power unleashed during the political crisis of the 1530s.

Late medieval procedural developments, which continued between 1485 and 1529, were simply hastened by the frenetic parliamentary activity and new-found powers of Reformation parliaments during the next thirty years. Procedures were neither a political instrument nor a means of acquiring power. They were simply devices for the efficient transaction of business. And as Parliament became more powerful, and popular, it became inundated with business. Power, and the volume of business, encouraged procedural innovations. The classic three-reading procedure for the enactment of laws was already taking shape before the Reformation [**doc. 3**]. By the accession of Elizabeth I (1558) it had become standardised, although anomalies and irregularities continued long afterwards. In its idealised form, bill procedure in each house followed a set pattern: each bill, entered on paper (see p. 38), had a literal first 'reading' of the text (because there were no printed copies for members to peruse at leisure); a second reading and debate on the bill's substance: scrutiny and (if necessary) amendment by a committee; engrossment on to parchment; and a final consideration confined to textual refinements [**doc. 3**]. If the Commons' procedural advances were more rapid than those in the Lords, that was simply because it was catching up with an older and more efficient, organised chamber.

The same was true of privileges. After all, the Upper House – consisting as it did of the King's enlarged Council of ecclesiastics and nobles, afforded by his professional counsel of law officers and judges – was closely associated with him. The Commons, however, enjoyed no such intimacy. It had to search out privileges which improved its effectiveness in law-making. That process passed through several stages. Whilst medieval Speakers requested that members should be exempt from arrest for civil suits, they were more concerned to obtain personal access to the King and to obtain his pardon if they misreported the proceedings of the House. In Henry VII's reign, however, they began to place more emphasis on the parliamentary privilege of the knights and burgesses. At the same time, the Commons displayed a growing interest in its collective 'liberties', which would enable it to carry out its duties more effectively. Early in the reign Strode's case[*] (1513) gave both its members and its actions protection from the law courts. This enlarged both individual privilege and the chamber's collective liberties. In 1515 a statute which empowered the Speaker to authorise (or refuse) the requests of members to absent themselves, allowed the House a degree of internal control, reinforced in 1550 when it also acquired the right to determine who could sit there [**doc. 7**]. Eight years later, in 1523, Sir Thomas More made the first recorded Speaker's request that each knight and burgess might speak freely, 'discharge his conscience' and offer his advice without fear [**doc. 4**]. By 1558 repeated requests of this kind were transforming the privilege into a cherished right. However, it was a right with two important limitations: that free speech was restricted to those great affairs placed before the House by the crown; and that it should not degenerate into disrespect for the monarch or his government. Nevertheless the growth of the Commons' privileges and liberties was nurtured by successive Tudor princes. When one of its number, George Ferrers, was arrested for debt in 1542, he was released by order of the House and not the Lord Chancellor, as had hitherto been customary. And Henry VIII endorsed the Commons action, declaring that he would not allow its privileges 'to be infringed in any point' (**56**, pp. 260–8; **62**, p.13).

Similarly, the crown did not intervene when the House questioned the credentials of those who had been elected [**doc. 7**]. These changes improved the Commons' efficiency. They were not politically inspired; nor did they constitute either a political maturation or 'rise' in its power, or a growing challenge to royal authority. The early Tudors remained in firm (and for the most part uncontested) control of Parliament. Furthermore the House of Lords – orderly, organised, socially superior and influential, beneficiary of the legal assistants' unequalled expertise – continued to be the more efficient, productive chamber. If it treated the 'Nether House' with more respect, now that it was a co-equal legislative partner, the latter continued to conduct itself with deference in its dealings with the lords spiritual and temporal. Disputes between the two Houses did occur, but they were the exception, not the rule. If the Commons made impressive advances between 1485 and 1558, it was simply trying to match its new responsibility with a greater business efficiency. Yet, when Mary died in 1558 it was still a much less organised chamber than the decorous House of Lords – and sometimes very disorderly.

4 Membership and Attendance

The Lords' membership

Whilst it is true to say that the House of Lords had become one chamber of a bicameral Parliament, this simple description does less than justice to its position within the institution. It was the historic nucleus of Parliament and it remained in possession of the Parliament House. Its seating arrangements – the throne, and beneath it the woolsacks which were occupied by the legal assistants and flanked by the benches of the bishops, abbots and nobles – were physical reminders of those early parliamentary occasions when the King, his Council and professional counsel met his great feudatories. This is why, in contrast to Continental assemblies, the two orders of clergy and nobles continued to deliberate and work together, when the knights and burgesses separated to form a Lower House (see pp. 1, 3). They did not serve as representatives of the first and second social estates. Instead, they were all summoned individually by virtue of their traditional relationship with the crown, both as men holding lands (baronies) directly from the King and as his natural Councillors. In 1515 the judges declared that the King could hold a Parliament without the lords spiritual because they 'had no place there except by reason of their temporal possessions' (**97**, p. 38). They did not sit as a separate order representing the interests of the Church (**56**, pp. 245–9). However, the original reason why particular men were summoned was in practice becoming less important. Some of the new nobility created by the early Tudors were not great landowners. And when Henry VIII, as supreme head of the Church, created six new bishoprics in 1540–2, he summoned their incumbents by virtue of their offices, not their possessions. Nevertheless, the new nobles owed their elevation to the crown [**doc. 5**] and, after the breach with Rome, the bishops were royal servants. Therefore the writs of summons which called them to the Lords continued to be an expression of their individual relationship with the monarch (**72**).

As a natural consequence of this relationship, it was the crown which had originally determined the Lords' membership (see p. 95) and royal actions were still an important influence in the early sixteenth century. For example, the crown varied the size and composition of the nobility, though rarely with a parliamentary motive in mind. On the one hand, it created new peers, but it also activated treason trials and, from 1534, parliamentary attainders without trial, both of which could lead to the termination of noble lines. In addition, the early Tudors sometimes granted, or sponsored in Parliament, the restitution in blood of a convicted traitor's heir, and even restored him to his father's noble dignity and a place in the Lords (**72**, Part 1). In contrast, until 1534, the King had no control over ecclesiastical organisation. After that date, however, the royal supreme head could and did reorganise the diocesan structure. Henry VIII added six bishoprics; Edward VI's government suppressed two and combined two more; and before Mary thankfully divested herself of the royal supremacy, she exercised it in order to reverse some of the Edwardian changes.

The crown still exercised a certain power to discriminate in the choice of those nobles who should be summoned to Parliament. However, customary practice and the identification of peerage (nobility) with the right to be summoned to the Lords (see p. 12) continued to narrow the King's freedom of choice. Henry VIII in particular respected the parliamentary rights of hereditary nobles. By doing so he gave additional impetus to the process whereby lordship of Parliament was recognised as the insignia of peerage [**doc. 5**]. But within the crown's now strictly circumscribed initiative, it could still exclude individuals for specific disabilities, such as minority, poverty, lunacy, royal detention or the priority of royal service elsewhere [**doc. 5**]. In addition, it had always enjoyed considerable discretion in the choice of the actual men who should serve as lords spiritual. The twenty-seven abbots and priors traditionally summoned were only 10 per cent of the existing regulars, and Henry VIII felt free to add two more early in his reign. Furthermore, in pre-Reformation England, the Pope consecrated the King's choice to vacant bishoprics as a matter of course. Even Thomas Cranmer was appointed in this collaborative way in 1533. Under the royal supremacy prelates were chosen by the King without reference to any foreign authority, and, upon Edward VI's accession in 1547, they were instructed to seek reappointment like any other royal official.

The turnover of Lords' personnel was accelerated in the rough-

and-tumble of Reformation politics, which were a mixture of fac-tional power-struggles and ideological conflict. Each reign produced its crop of aristocratic victims and purges of the episcopal bench, together with the ennoblement of loyal servants and the consecration of bishops of the right religious complexion. The result was the fre-quent removal of familiar faces and the appearance of new ones in the many parliaments of 1529–58. The one sweeping alteration was the elimination of the parliamentary regulars when the monasteries were dissolved in 1536–40. Most of these changes were not made in order to produce a more reliable and supportive House of Lords. The nobles who suffered execution were usually guilty of treason or the victims of vicious faction politics, whilst Henry VIII, Edward VI's governors, and Mary I all required bishops who were of their persuasion and would be the vanguard of their religious policies (see the case of Bishop Taylor [**doc. 5**]). And of course the departure of the abbots and priors was the automatic consequence of the Dis-solution. There remain two important exceptions. Stephen Gar-diner, Bishop of Winchester, the most dangerous opponent of the Edwardian Protestant Reformation, was imprisoned during the first three sessions of the young King's opening Parliament (1547–50) and then deprived [**docs. 5, 30**]. In the next reign, Edward Cour-tenay, Earl of Devon, was the figurehead of a rebellion which, in early 1554, attempted to frustrate Mary's marriage to Philip of Spain. Gardiner was removed, because of the parliamentary 'stirs' which he could cause. Devon's imprisonment (1554–5) and exile abroad (1555–6) prevented him from being a parliamentary focus of anti-Spanish sentiment. These cases apart, however, individual peers or prelates were not penalised with Parliament in mind.

Indeed, apart from the regulars' removal, the composition of the Upper House was affected more by the normal rhythms of early modern existence. Noble sons replaced fathers, vacant bishoprics were filled, deaths terminated peerages, grateful monarchs rewarded loyal subjects with noble titles, promotions to higher noble rank, or summonses to their heirs who were called to the Lords in their father's junior titles [**doc. 5**]. Kaleidoscopic Reformation politics simply magnified and accelerated the process of change caused by natural wastage and royal beneficence. Whatever the causes, three significant changes occurred in the Lords' membership under the first four Tudors. The late medieval nobility was already a rural-based, landed plutocracy, few of whose families could claim ancient pedigree and title. But, by Elizabeth's accession, the nobility had acquired an even more distinct *nouveau* quality. Almost half of the families had been raised to the peerage since 1485, and many of the remainder had been promoted to their current titles by the early Tudors. Secondly, the regulars' removal in the later 1530s effectively secularised the House of Lords. Thereafter, at least until 1558, the bishops, fluctuating between twenty-four and twenty-seven, were outnumbered by between forty-three and fifty lords temporal. At the same time, the parliamentary effect of the Dissolution of the Monasteries was a shrinkage of the Lords' membership, by more than 25 per cent. Mary I's addition of a solitary abbot and the lay prior of Saint John of Jerusalem, together with the crown's occasional exercise of its right to call up the heir of a senior living peer in one of his father's lesser titles, had minimal effect. By 1558 the Upper House was small, and its membership dominated by a nobility which was largely plutocratic, and of recent, Tudor-appointed origin (**60**).

The Commons' membership and the significance of the patron–client relationship

Whereas the Lords' membership diminished in size, the early Tudor Commons grew from 296 to 400 – an increase of more than a third. Until 1529 the membership remained static. The dramatic expansion occurred thereafter. The enfranchisement of Calais [**doc. 7**], which ended with its capture by the French in 1558, and of Wales and the marcher (border) counties of Cheshire and Monmouthshire, were part and parcel of the State-building process in the 1530s. At the same time English borough representation was enlarged: by fourteen members under Henry VIII, thirty-four under Edward VI and a further twenty-five under Mary I. As the crown alone exercised the power to enfranchise, it might be assumed that its motive was to increase the presence of its servants in the Commons. After all, many of the additions were small boroughs, naturally more susceptible to outside pressures and influences. The Edwardian creations were Cornish ports, where crown influence, exercised through its Duchy of Cornwall administration, could determine elections. And some of the Marian additions were in the conservative north.

However, the revisionists have argued that the Tudors, far from attempting to manipulate the electoral system to their own, possibly sinister, ends, were themselves under pressure. The parliamentary appetite of the socially dominant elite of landed peers and gentlemen, who had already narrowed the shire franchise to their own advantage, was not satisfied by the relatively small number of county seats. They were continuing the invasion of parliamentary boroughs which they had begun in the fifteenth century (see p. 12). Under the early Tudors the pace increased as the gentry swarmed into the urban constituencies [**doc. 8**]. They held out the inducement of parliamentary service without wages – an inducement which many of the smaller and impoverished boroughs found irresistible (**73**, Chapter 7). Behind many of these carpet-bagging gentlemen were great noble patrons such as the Duke of Buckingham and the west-country Courtenays before 1529; Norfolk, Arundel and Bedford [**doc. 9**] during the turbulent Reformation decades; and the occasional politicking bishop such as Stephen Gardiner (Winchester). These men were not just political puppet masters, tugging electoral strings to hoist into the Commons those of their creatures who would advance their religious causes and personal interests. Of course it was to their advantage to persuade the monarch to enfranchise yet another borough which would return their nominees: such achievements enhanced their social stature, as did their successful (albeit more discreet) interventions in shire elections. At the same time they, no less than the crown, were under pressure to enlarge the parliamentary opportunities for the loyalist gentlemen who looked to them for advancement.

The revisionist explanation provides only a partial truth. Loach has shown that Henrician creations were sometimes motivated by royal needs in a time of extended crisis (**109**), and the same was true in the two succeeding reigns. It would have been irresponsible, indeed unnatural, for royal government not to exploit every possible source of support as it tried to push through parliamentary programmes of radical change (or reaction). Likewise Privy Councillors and other royal servants were not (indeed could not afford to be) laggards in the matter. They too went 'borough hunting' in order to sit in the Commons and serve their royal master or mistress there. On the other hand, Loach's treatment of parliaments as political assemblies, concerned with great issues, should not blind us to the fact that they were also socio-economic mechanisms, designed to benefit all kinds of interests in the upper tiers of society.

The demand for parliamentary seats cannot be explained in simple Whiggish or revisionist terms. As the Commons emerged as a fully integrated part of Parliament, and a co-equal partner of the Lords in the legislative process, it was natural for the crown to extend its managerial network. The anxiety of royal servants to sit there, however, did not mark the political rise of the Lower House. It was a judicious response by Tudor monarchs, who were sensibly concerned to control all organs of the contemporary political machine. If it now required two Houses to make a law, then both must be managed. Secondly, the Commons' new institutional status made membership a mark of personal status for gentlemen, and part of the socio-political apprenticeship which would fit them to govern their local communities. For many, especially aspiring lawyers, a loyal and able parliamentary performance might launch them on a career in royal service. Thirdly, the invasion of boroughs by carpet-bagging gentry did not usually arouse resentment amongst the inhabitants. The electoral system was designed to represent organic communities, not individuals. It did not matter how members were chosen or, indeed, where they came from, but whether they represented effectively the interests of their communities in the Lower House. Finally, the establishment of a permanent gentry majority in the Commons was the consequence of the rise of a rural landed elite to socio-political dominance in the kingdom. Peers and gentlemen enjoyed a common social outlook, the same economic priorities, and a shared determination to maintain their supremacy under the crown. When a noble patron secured a gentleman-client's election for a parliamentary borough, it was no more than the performance of two different roles by members of the same homogeneous governing class.

The results of this development were equally clearcut. The Lower House, like the Upper, came to represent the dominant group in the community. There were notable exceptions, such as the representatives from the rich and powerful merchants of London, Bristol, Norwich and York. These exceptions apart, however, the change in the Commons' social composition also reflected the growth in the nobles' parliamentary influence. The emergence of a bicameral Parliament magnified rather than diminished the nobles' role. Many of their kin, friends, allies and clients now sat in the Lower House. Their electoral influence simply added to the nobles' stock of patronage and therefore to their socio-political status and influence.

Attendance and absenteeism

The deficient, sometimes even fragmentary, nature of the early modern parliamentary record cannot conceal the fact that the search for seats in the Commons was not matched by a willingness to turn up regularly and shoulder the burden of business. Admittedly it was tedious work: lengthy debate; hours passed listening to the text of bills intoned by the clerk; or time spent in committee rooms laboriously scrutinising and revising proposed new laws. Parliamentary drudgery contributed to the perennial problem of absenteeism. The Act of 1515, empowering the Speaker and House to authorise the departure of members from Westminster during the session, was an early attempt to deal with it [**doc. 11**]. The timing of the Act is significant. There had been frequent sessions during the past five years. Each one disrupted the personal lives of members, who were faced with long journeys, expensive London lodgings, the risk of disease, and later the task of extracting parliamentary wages from reluctant boroughs. That frequent sessions encouraged absenteeism is amply illustrated during the many parliaments between 1529 and 1558. Official attempts to combat the problem included roll calls of members, a bill to penalise unauthorised truants (1548/9), and even, in 1555, legal proceedings and fines [**doc. 11**]. There is no way of determining what success these measures enjoyed, but such evidence as exists points to official failure. Absenteeism was endemic and, in Mary I's reign, it was exacerbated by the unpopularity of some of her policies.

The fuller records of the House of Lords, in particular the Clerk's daily attendance register from 1515 onwards, permit a more precise evaluation of absenteeism there. J. S. Roskell charted the variable, often poor (and in the case of the regulars lamentable) attendance record of the late medieval upper chamber (see p. 13). Threats of punishment and the imposition of fines had made no difference. Although unauthorised absentees were again fined in 1515, Henry VIII's early parliaments did not show a marked improvement (**72**, pp 120–1). A mere handful of peers turned up regularly. Many failed to appear at all. And the regulars continued to default in large numbers, though on most days the lords spiritual maintained their paper majority in practice as well (**61**, pp. 49–50). The crown attempted to regulate absenteeism from the Lords, in much the same way as it did, with the Act of 1515, for the Lower House. A member who wished to stay away because of illness, expense, or age, or who might be required to perform other royal service in the Parliament time [**doc. 6**], applied to the King or one of his ministers for a licence of absence. If it was granted, the licensee was required to nominate one or more proctors who would exercise his voice in his absence. The purpose of the procedure was twofold. It enabled the King to regulate attendance, whilst it confirmed both the duty and right of lords spiritual and temporal to attend. In practice, the crown adopted a rather relaxed attitude to absenteeism. On any given day the King's noble Councillors might attend his Council but not Parliament, which was just a short walk away. Some members did not bother to sue out a licence but stayed away nonetheless. Although others dutifully obtained permission to do so and named proctors, the practice of proctorial representation itself had no practical significance. Proctors could not exercise a vote on behalf of absentees and, moreover, they were often absent themselves (**61**, pp. 49–51, 71, 74–6, **111**).

The apparent lack of consistent royal pressure on members to attend ended in the critical years of the 1530s, and especially during Thomas Cromwell's supremacy. He monitored applications for licences, advised Henry VIII (in 1536) to grant few of them, whilst at the same time instructing political opponents not to come [**doc. 12**]. Despite the burden of frequent sessions and increased cries to be spared [**doc. 6**], Cromwell's assiduous attention to detail bore fruit (**72**, pp. 120, 124). The Lords' attendance record in 1536 and 1539–40 was the best in the reign. Thereafter, however, with the fall of Cromwell (1540) and the involvement of many nobles in the renewed wars with Scotland and France, absenteeism rose sharply. In contrast, the Edwardian parliaments registered a return to the high Cromwellian level. This was, to some extent, a consequence of the King's minority, because his government was managed by nobles who felt obliged to attend. But it was also because the Council continued to scrutinise members' obligations, instructing some to stay at their posts and ordering others to attend [**doc. 12**]. In addition, the front-line battles of the Edwardian Reformation were fought out in the Upper House, between Protestant and Catholic bishops and peers. Mary I's administration was concerned to ensure the same high level of attendance, because the Queen was convinced of the importance of the nobility's role in the parliamentary enactment of her Spanish and Catholic policies. But those policies were divisive. So were the faction-ridden politics of her Council and, in particular, the polarising rivalry of Bishop Gardiner and Lord Paget. Their conflicts were transferred to the floors of the two troubled and troublesome Houses of her parliaments (see pp. 72–6) and, together with the unpopularity of Marian policies, contributed to the growth of irregular attendance and sessional absenteeism during the reign.

5 The Business Record of Early Tudor Parliaments

Official business and public Acts

The statutes enacted by the early Tudor parliaments all had equal force in law. However, they differed in kind, scope, and origin. Some were 'beneficial' Acts, which bestowed advantages on an individual, a community, or an occupational group. Others were 'penal' and imposed punishments. Acts were also public or private. To some extent this was a technical distinction, determined by the necessity (or otherwise) of paying fees to the parliamentary clerks. Such payments identified a bill as private, but if none were required then it was designated as public. However, once a private measure had negotiated the shoals and rapids of the two Houses, it might be upgraded to public status by payment of a fee to the Clerk of the Parliaments. He would then enrol it as such on the Parliament Roll. Nevertheless, the distinction generally holds true that public Acts were laws of general application, affecting the whole community, whilst private Acts were not. Finally, it is important to make the general distinction between official measures of royal origin and public Acts. Many bills promoted by the crown were designed to apply throughout the kingdom: for example, grants of taxation, security measures, additions or modifications to the criminal code, poor laws and other commonweal legislation. However, some official proposals submitted to Parliament touched only the monarch, members of his family, or particular royal estates.

Similarly, attainders of traitors and the forfeiture of their property to the crown were confirmed by statute, especially in the case of prominent Yorkists in Henry VII's reign. From 1534 onwards rebels, conspirators, some heretics, other opponents of royal policies, and several victims of Henry VIII's personal displeasure were actually condemned by Act of Parliament without proceeding to trial: for example, Elizabeth Barton (the 'Nun of Kent') in 1534, the Countess of Salisbury (1539), Thomas Cromwell, Earl of Essex (1540), and the Duke of Norfolk (1547) (**38**, pp. 59–60; **56**, pp. 80–2; **72**, Chapter 2; **84**, pp. 378–80).

Condemnation for treason not only deprived the traitor of his life, property and his peerage dignity (if any). It also corrupted the blood of his heirs, who were thereby disabled from holding any title or honour in the future. Frequently, especially during the religious and political changes of the Reformation decades, monarchs acceded to the heirs' petitions for their restitution in blood. This was normally done by a bill couched in petitionary form, written on parchment not paper (see p. 27), and bearing the royal sign manual (signature) when it was submitted to Parliament. There were, for example, thirty-two Acts of restitution between 1547 and 1558. Of these, sixteen restored in blood attainted peers, their heirs or other relatives, and in four cases noble title as well (**60**, pp. 12–13). It should be added that royal support of the parliamentary bills of individuals, publicly demonstrated by the use of the sign manual, was not confined to restitutions. These measures, known as bills of grace, included exchanges of land with the King, property settlements, and other matters relating to the estates of prominent families. In all of these cases – attainders (and confirmations thereof) and bills of grace – the motivating force or sponsor was the King and in this sense they were 'official'. But they affected only particular individuals and families and in no sense could they be designated public Acts of general application.

Conversely, in the parliaments of all the early Tudors, private members promoted bills which were public and general in their scope. Amongst the more prominent examples were the political 'backlash' against the supposed extortion and other financial misdeeds of Henry VII's government, in the first Parliament of his son's reign (1510) (**55**, pp. 35–6); and reforms of common-law procedures, often promoted by concerned lawyers. Most notable, even notorious, was the campaign against social and economic injustice mounted by John Hales in the Edwardian Parliament in 1548–9. Hales' parliamentary attack on the financial greed and self-interest of the governing class, which he divined as the basic cause of the current hectic inflation, included proposed laws both against the enclosure and conversion of arable land to pasture and the rapid purchase and re-sale of cattle by entrepreneurs, as well as a tax on sheep and wool. G. R. Elton accurately identified Hales as 'that notable example of the confident economic expert who gets it all wrong'. More pertinent here is the fact that, whilst Protector Somerset lent sympathetic and constructive support to the idealistic but wrong-headed Hales, it was Hales and not the Protector who was the author of the commonweal programme of bills. Its chances of parliamentary success were nil, because it was inimical to power-ful governing-class interests, and three specific measures failed be-cause of lack of assistance from the Privy Council (**55**, pp. 343–5).

Nevertheless, as parliaments were called to service royal govern-ment, there was always a corpus of official legislation which was national in scope and impact. The most frequent reason for the sum-moning of yet another assembly was financial assistance – in other words 'supply'. This was particularly true in wartime, but that was not the case in the reign of Henry VII, who pursued a neutralist, even isolationist, and therefore financially cheap foreign policy. However, his intention to secure the new dynasty and revive strong monarchy could not be realised without the rejuvenation of the late medieval crown's depleted financial resources. Henry's attack was two-pronged. First, he searched out the limits of the crown's hereditary revenues: the income from royal estates; feudal 'incidents' (the payments due to him as feudal overlord) – in particular wardship, the profitable guardianship of the person and estates of minors who were the King's tenants-in-chief; and ill-defined (and therefore exploitable) prerogative rights, such as the issue of pardons and of bonds for good behaviour. He also levied forced loans (which he later repaid) and a benevolence (theoretically a gift donated out of love and devotion) from his wealthier subjects. Secondly, he turned to parliaments. In accordance with the precedent set in Richard III's reign, Henry received a life-grant of tunnage and poundage (additional customs duties) from his first Parliament in 1485. Thereafter he sought and received fifteenths and tenths (taxes on personal property) in 1487, 1489, 1491 and 1497. He was granted a poll tax on merchants trading into England (1487). Then in 1489 he experimented with an income tax on the laity and re-peated it in the parliaments of 1497 and 1504. This was the forerunner of the subsidy, which was to become the Tudors' staple parliamentary tax. Moreover the 1495 assembly gave retrospective approval to his benevolence of 1491, despite the fact that a statute of Richard III's reign had made such impositions illegal. And when, in 1504, Henry sought two feudal aids he was offered a sum only a little less than he had requested.

The picture presented thus far is one of parliamentary co-operation and royal success. However, it must be modified in several important particulars. The first experiment with the subsidy produced only a small yield and a tax rebellion. Since the mid-four-teenth century, fifteenths and tenths had become fixed contribu-tions, which were never adjusted to allow for inflation or the growing

wealth of many taxpayers. And Henry's request for feudal aids*
probably provoked the resistance of the Commons [**doc. 13**]. Instead, the Lower House voted a subsidy, which the King reduced
by a quarter, perhaps to soothe ruffled tempers (**38**, pp. 25–8,
53–7).

By 1504 Henry VII could afford such a diplomatic gesture. As he
secured his position on the throne, restored a modicum of law and
order, and restored the crown to solvency, his need for parliaments
lessened: five met in the first decade of the reign, but only two during
the last fourteen years. His declaration of 1504, that he would not
call another Parliament for a long time, was not just a politician's
platitude. When members next rode into Westminster, it was to attend the first assembly of his son's reign, in 1510. Henry VIII's
bellicose foreign policy produced an immediate and dramatic transformation: frequent sessions (six between 1510 and 1515), and
heavy, regular financial demands. A modern estimate of the tax-
yield resulting from these parliaments puts it at £287,000 over a five-
year period, excluding the poll tax of 1513 (**46**, p. 119). In contrast
Henry VII received only a little more (£312,000) from subsidies and
fifteenths and tenths* during his entire reign of twenty-four years
(**38**, p. 55n[1]). The rise of Thomas Wolsey, who became the chief
manager of Henry VIII's affairs, Archbishop of York (1514), Lord
Chancellor (1515) and papal legate (1518), produced a parliamentary hiatus. Wolsey's autocratic temper did not respond well to
criticism, especially after the Commons' virulent attack on the clergy
and its privileges in 1515. However, he was the King's war minister
and, by 1523, Henry's costly foreign policy necessitated the calling
of yet another Parliament. By then the crown was in sore financial
straits, yet neither the King nor his chief minister could expect a
sympathetic parliamentary response. Coin was in short supply in
the kingdom – considerably less than two million pounds, of which
£260,000 was collected by the loan of 1522–3. Therefore it is not
surprising that Wolsey's request for a tax, which, at the rate of
four shillings in the pound, was optimistically designed to raise
£800,000, provoked a bitter and resentful response in the Commons
[**doc. 25**]. Eventually, after debate stretching over a fortnight, the
cardinal settled for a subsidy of two shillings in the pound, payable
in two annual instalments, as well as the confirmation of a clerical
tax of unprecedented size (**46**, pp. 116–23).

The next Parliament (1529) met after Wolsey's downfall, and in
response to Henry's pressing and related matrimonial and succession problems. Some of the statutes which the King sought and

obtained, in the critical decade which followed, were not directed specifically to these ends, but were financial in purpose: for example, the transference of the papal taxes on the clergy, known as first fruits and tenths, to the crown (1534); the Statute of Uses in 1536 (see pp. 69–70), and the Dissolution of the Monasteries (1536 and 1539). Occasionally Henry also applied to Parliament for a tax. However, it was still a convention, even if it was not a constitutional principle, that the crown should manage on its hereditary revenues, except in time of actual or impending war. Although in 1529 a peace-time Parliament cancelled the King's obligation to repay earlier forced loans [**doc. 28**], they had been raised when England was at war and, in any case, they did not constitute a new tax. In contrast, in 1532 the government abandoned an attempt to obtain a fifteenth and tenth* because of Commons' opposition. When it received a modest grant in 1534, tax evasion and resistance were widespread, and another request in 1539 ended in total failure. However, the subsidy bill of 1540 was masterminded by the King's chief parliamentary draftsman and architect, Thomas Cromwell. Not only was it successful, but, together with the tax of 1534, it introduced an important new principle: that taxation was justified in peacetime as well as in war. The formal justification, set forth in the officially drafted preamble of each subsidy bill, was the obligation on the part of subjects to show their gratitude for the benefits of Henry VIII's rule. The real and more prosaic reason was that inflation, together with the growth in the functions and activity of royal government, had rendered the crown's hereditary revenues inadequate (**98**).

As might be expected, the parliamentary classes who footed the financial bill did not accept, immediately or slavishly, this innovatory principle. In any case, Cromwell fell in 1540 and the remaining parliaments of Henry's reign were called on to fund his renewed wars with Scotland and France. These cost an unprecedented 2–3 million (**46**, p. 53). In 1543 and 1545, the demand for parliamentary taxation, which contributed £430,000 (**55**, pp. 310–11), was justified on the traditional ground of military needs. The same was true in Edward VI's reign, when Protector Somerset invaded Scotland. His expensive and ultimately disastrous military adventure, coupled with Henry VIII's war debts, could not be funded out of hereditary royal revenues. Somerset obtained the parliamentary dissolution of the chantries (foundations endowed to say masses for their benefactors) and their transfer to the crown (1547), followed by a levy on sheep, wool and cloth in 1548/9. However, these could also be justified on other grounds: the former as a blow for 'true religion' and the latter as a commonweal measure against those who caused depopulation and unemployment in the countryside by converting arable land to pasture. Equally significant, but carefully concealed, was the lavish distribution of royal property amongst the ruling clique – a process which progressively impoverished the crown. When in 1553 Somerset's successor, the Duke of Northumberland, summoned Edward VI's last Parliament in the King's name, he could hardly present military expenditure as the justification for a subsidy. Instead, the advancement of Protestantism and the restoration of the 'decayed house' of the commonwealth loomed large in the preamble. Northumberland remained nervous about the Commons' response. Himself a major beneficiary of the continued plundering of royal resources, he emphasised to other Councillors that no mention should be made of the King's gifts 'in augmentation or advancing of his nobles, or . . . good servants' [**doc. 28**]. Mary I also made just one peace-time request for taxation, in 1555, and the subsidy preamble likewise followed the Cromwellian model. Thus successive financially-straitened governments laid the foundations on which Elizabeth I built as she regularly applied to parliaments for money in time of peace and almost as a matter of course.

Whilst parliaments were often called primarily for supply, this was by no means always the case. Almost half the sessions (twenty-two out of forty-seven) held in the reigns of the first four Tudors were called without money in mind. The first parliament of a new monarch was a public-relations exercise. Of course it performed the very important financial service of voting a life grant of tunnage and poundage (additional customs duties). Nevertheless, its prime purpose was to advertise the new regime and enable the King to make acquaintance with the nobility, great clergy, and representatives of the rural and urban communities. As parliaments became more self-confident and skilled in their legislative function, monarchs increasingly looked to Lords and Commons for the passing of laws in the interest of good governance. And, when necessary, they sought out governing-class opinion on matters of great moment, as their royal predecessors had done for more than two centuries. In an age of poor communications, what better opportunity could be afforded them than the occasion of a Parliament? Henry VII demonstrated this when he both canvassed loyalty for the *nouveau* Tudor dynasty and buttressed it with statutory bulwarks. The declaration of his royal title (1485), attainders of his Yorkist enemies, and the *de facto*

Act of 1495, which protected from later punishment those who were loyal to a reigning king, were all designed to secure the position of Henry and his heirs [**doc. 1**]. The so-called Star Chamber Act (1487), which dealt with both the causes of public disorder and judicial corruption, and measures reinforcing the authority of local magistrates and penalising magnates who kept armed retainers or private armies, were intended to restore order after the fifteenth-century civil wars.

Henry VII utilised the law-making authority of parliaments to achieve a settled order and so justify his acquisition of power. His son used it to launch the kingdom along a rapid, dramatic, even revolutionary, course of change (**53, 55, 56**). Henry VIII's search for dynastic stability provided the initial parliamentary impetus between 1529 and 1533. The momentum of change released by this royal impulse, and skilfully translated into practical results by royal servants, above all by Thomas Cromwell, was then maintained throughout the 1530s. Whether or not the events of the 1530s warrant the label 'revolution' matters little here. During the past thirty years historians have consumed much time and print, and misdirected much energy, on the semantics of change (**51, 92, 93, 104, 105**). Far more important are the role of Parliament in the process of change and the consequences of its participation, both for the institution itself and for the authority of statute (see pp. 26–7).

The Reformation Parliament (1529–36) was called first for advice on the King's 'great matter', then to assist him both to reduce the English clergy to obedience (the Act for the Pardon of the Clergy in 1532) and to apply pressure on the Pope to decree the annulment of his first marriage (the Act in Conditional Restraint of Annates, also in 1532). Finally, when the unyielding stance of the papacy drove Henry to more drastic courses, these were also pursued through Parliament. The Act in Restraint of Appeals (1533) enabled Archbishop Cranmer to annul Henry's marriage and disbarred Catherine from appealing to Rome. In the following year a series of statutes removed England from allegiance to the Pope, whose powers were transferred to the crown. One of these statutes, the Act of Supremacy, acknowledged Henry as the supreme head of a national Catholic Church. Nor was that the end of Parliament's work. In the interests of State security and in defence of the new Church, Henry was empowered to proceed against traitors, heretics and papal supporters. The energy, bureaucratic tidiness and political vision of his chief minister, Thomas Cromwell, spawned further legislation. The concept of England as an 'empire' – a sovereign national State independent of all other earthly authorities – was enunciated in the preamble to the Act in Restraint of Appeals. The idea was not new, nor did it originate with Cromwell, but its insertion there was his doing (**91**). To give it reality, the authority of the King must be effective everywhere. So statutes suppressed the semi-autonomous franchises (1536), and the monastic orders which took an oath of allegiance to the Pope (1536 and 1539). Wales and the Welsh border areas (known as 'marches') were 'shired' (divided into counties) and given English justice and law courts (1536 and 1543). Additional funding for the new State was provided by transferring to it first fruits and tenths (paid by the clergy to the Pope until 1534) and monastic property. Parliament also invalidated the use (trust) and so guaranteed the King's right to all feudal dues (see pp. 69–70), and in 1545 empowered him to dissolve chantries.

This parliamentary productivity was not achieved without criticism and even, in the early 1530s, signs of organised opposition (see pp. 66–7). Nevertheless the range, volume and importance of the official business successfully transacted can be attributed to the high degree of co-operation between King, Lords and Commons, and to parliamentary acquiescence in royal designs. Repeatedly it delegated legislative authority to Henry: for example, the right to enforce the Act in Restraint of Annates and the union of Wales and England, to alter the succession, and to dissolve chantries as and when he chose. And in 1539, after a good deal of debate and amendment, it backed the enforcement of proclamations with statutory authority (**55**, pp. 285–6). At the same time the King and his ministers showed an inclination to refer all important proposals for change to Parliament, even Cromwell's bureaucratic reorganisation of government departments, which required no such sanction (**52**). Those statutes which dealt with administrative restructuring signified royal and ministerial confidence in Parliament. Resort to it, first for resolution of the King's 'great matter', and then for all the changes which followed in its train, was not the result of some brilliant political insight on the part of Henry VIII or his minister. The institution, as the public forum of the governing elite, was the only place where Henry could secure that elite's support, and it provided the only mechanism which could give legal force to his actions. There was no alternative to a parliamentary solution of the King's problems.

After Cromwell's fall in 1540, Henry continued to refer urgent causes to Parliament. The great codifying statute for Wales (1543), the final arrangements for the succession (1544), the Chantries Act, the continuation of changes in the central administration, and a spate of law reforms all post-dated Cromwell's death. Furthermore, the King continued to use Parliament in religious matters. The spread of Protestant heresy and the threat of a Catholic crusade against schismatic England were disturbing legacies from the 1530s. Although the Act of Supremacy of 1534 recognised the King as supreme head of the Church, with the power to determine doctrine, he continued to defer to Parliament, in order to bolster the exercise of his authority. Examples of this are the Act of Six Articles (1539), and later measures dealing with the punishment of non-conformity and the use of the vernacular Bible.

Until the end of Henry's reign, parliaments continued to be collaborative ventures in which a self-assured King was able to get more or less what he wanted – perhaps because experience had taught him the limits beyond which he should not trespass on the goodwill of his 'faithful' Lords and Commons. The accession of Edward VI brought a dramatic political and parliamentary transformation. The aristocratic regimes of the Dukes of Somerset and Northumberland lacked the self-confidence of Henry's rule and were more vulnerable than a monarch ruling in his own right to criticism and opposition. This was expressed in a number of ways. Grace bills bearing the sign manual* were endorsed by Councillors and judges, because a minor's signature might not be regarded as good in law. Secondly, the Privy Council's bills did not seek delegated legislative powers. Thirdly, whereas Parliament had not made Henry VIII supreme head but simply acknowledged him as such, the religious changes inaugurated by Edward's aristocratic governors, and incorporated in statute, were all enacted explicitly by 'authority of Parliament'. Moreover, the Henrician Act empowering the young King to repeal any laws passed during his minority was itself annulled. In all these ways, Edwardian aristocratic government diminished the crown's legislative authority. It also conceded to the Lords and Commons the power to veto any future alteration in religion which the crown might propose.

At the same time, official bills continued to occupy much of Parliament's time. Protector Somerset set the tone during his brief ascendancy (1547–9). He was dubbed the 'good duke' by historians such as A. F. Pollard and W. K. Jordan (**66, 76**), but more recent research has shown him to be politically inept, naive, self-seeking and corrupt. His omnibus Act of 1547 repealed many (though not all) of the penal and deterrent statutes enacted in Henry VIII's reign and earlier, including some new Henrician treasons, the Proclamations Act, and older heresy laws. It was a shortsighted measure which robbed a vulnerable regime of some important defensive weapons. Moreover, Edwardian England was a disturbed society, wracked by religious division and economic dislocation. It was not long before the government had to secure new laws to deal with vagabondage and public disturbances, in particular the Act against Unlawful Public Assemblies (1549–50). Somerset's decision to permit the parliamentary attainder and execution of his brother, Thomas Seymour, in 1548/9, proved a political error. His mismanagement of royal revenues, and the exorbitant cost of his Scottish war, resulted in an early, frantic, and continuing search for revenue. And the assets deriving from the 1547 Act to dissolve chantries (few of which had been suppressed by Henry VIII under the terms of the 1545 statute) were rapidly frittered away.

The regime of Somerset's successor, Northumberland, did not mark a decline in the quality of government. Northumberland was more ruthless, but he also had more political acumen. He withdrew from Scottish and Continental involvement. In 1549–50 he secured from Parliament harsh measures in defence of public order. Building on the moderate Protestant innovations sponsored by Somerset in the sessions of 1547 and 1548/9, he patronised a more thoroughgoing Reformation. So the prayer book and order of worship, enacted in 1549 but full of ambiguities and Catholic vestiges, were replaced by an uncompromisingly Protestant version in 1552 – once again enacted by parliamentary authority. The government had obtained the laws which it wanted, although, as we have seen, in the process it had lost its initiative and power to act independently of Parliament in the alteration of religion.

The discontinuity between government requirements in the Edwardian and in the Marian parliaments is obvious. Whereas Edward's governors had used Parliament to enact a Protestant Reformation into law, Mary sought the statutory restoration of the Catholic faith under papal supremacy. Yet there was also a common denominator. The Edwardian Church, created by parliamentary statute, could be destroyed and replaced only by the same means. However, religious alteration was not a simple matter which could be encompassed in a single Act of Parliament. Doctrine, the order of worship, the competence of ecclesiastical courts, the authority and religious opinions of the clergy, papal power and taxes, laws against heresy, and the vexed question of confiscated Church property: all required bills to be drawn and subjected to parliamentary scrutiny. The Queen's marriage to Philip of Spain in

1554 produced more official measures: ratification of the marriage treaty (1554), protection of her consort by the treason laws*, and confirmation of his governorship of their children if she predeceased him (1554–5). And when he persuaded Mary to align England with Spain in war against France, much of Parliament's time in 1558 was devoted to official measures concerned with security, military organisation and funding: for example, Acts 'for the having of horse armour and weapons', for troop musters, for the investigation of the behaviour of French residents in England, and for clerical and lay subsidies. In addition it considered six other military bills and three more of a xenophobic, anti-French nature. There was also a crop of parliamentary confirmations of attainder, after Northumberland's attempt to divert the succession (1553), and Thomas Wyatt's unsuccessful anti-Spanish rebellion (1554), as well as a batch of restitutions, most notably of Edward Courtenay (see p. 73), the Duke of Norfolk, and Cardinal Pole. Despite some opposition and occasional setbacks, and with the important exception of the return of expropriated property to the Church, almost the entire Marian legislative programme passed into law. The Queen's preference for short sessions, reinforced by the contentious nature of some of her policies (see pp. 72–5) and the number and complexity of official bills, tended to squeeze out the measures promoted by local communities, corporations, and individuals. Her objectives preoccupied Parliament and its time to an extent not known before, even in her father's reign.

Beneficial laws for the localities, corporations, economic lobbies and individuals

The distinction between the official and private authorship of bills was often obscured by parliamentary politicking. Royal government sometimes gave its support to the sponsors of legislative proposals which it had not drafted. These measures ranged from the unrealistic schemes of John Hales during Somerset's protectorate, to the bills of hard-headed local and economic lobbies. Grace bills, bearing the sign manual and benefiting particular individuals, were the most obvious example of royal favour. But frequently a Privy Councillor, persuaded by the worthiness of a cause, or accompanying *douceurs**, succumbed to canvassing and lent his voice and prestige in support of a private measure. The promoters of such measures, especially London which had the most organised lobby of all, were prepared to go even higher, seeking the Lord Chancellor's support and, in

1523 for example, even petitioning the King. This kind of activity is a reminder that there were two parties involved in the parliamentary process: not only the crown which called Parliament into existence for its own purposes, but also governing-class interests which exploited the occasion to their own advantage. In short, Parliament enacted laws which embodied the aspirations and needs of all sorts and conditions of men (and of women too, though only if they were very wealthy, influential or well-connected). Powerful families and great men were able to plead their causes at the bar of the two Houses [**doc. 14**]. In 1553, when the Duke of Norfolk's restitution bill was held up by disputes with those who had acquired some of his property since his attainder six years earlier, he made a personal appearance before the Commons. Norfolk asked the House to pass his bill, remit the property dispute to impartial arbiters and, if there was still no agreement, 'then the Queen to make a final end' (**32**, vol. 1, p. 32). Conversely, when in 1552 the Duke of Northumberland sought to deprive and attaint Bishop Tunstal of Durham, the Commons refused to proceed because the accused was denied permission to appear at the bar in his own defence. Parliament displayed a similar tender concern for the fallen Protector Somerset in 1549–50. Before passing the bill for his 'fine and ransom', it took appropriate action to reassure itself that his confession of his faults had been voluntary and not 'enforced'; it examined his dispute with Lord Audley; and, as a consequence, when the bill finally passed into law, it was endorsed by the Duke and his wife, as well as by the King and his Councillors.

Just as great individuals sought, and sometimes received, satisfaction at Parliament's hands, so did local communities and corporations. The extent to which this occurred is difficult to chart for much of the period. As most of the failed bills, drafted on paper, were destroyed in the great parliamentary fire of the nineteenth century, our knowledge of them depends on their appearance in the business journals of the two Houses. However, the Lords' Journal is extant only from 1510 – and then with substantial gaps – whilst the surviving Commons' record does not commence until 1547. Nevertheless, it is possible to make some observations and to reach a number of tentative conclusions about the legislative input of private interests under the first four Tudors. First, the range of legislation in the parliaments of Henry VII was as wide in subject and geographical range as it was to be in succeeding reigns. It covered public order and access of the poor to justice; hunting at night or in disguise; fairs, markets and the cloth trade; coinage, weights and mesures, and trading standards; wages and hours of work; and that perennial scapegoat, the vagabond. Parliament also passed measures dealing with borough affairs from Newcastle to London (**38**, pp. 60–2). Whilst it is impossible to determine who initiated most of these bills, many benefited men of substance and must have been promoted by them. Despite the priority given by the government to war-funding in 1510–15, Parliament was not deterred from consideration of bills on bridges, river boatmen, leather, wool and the regulation of dress in accordance with social status (known as sumptuary laws*). And, as the government's legislative horizons widened in the sessions of the 1530s, so did the volume of private business. Peers, gentry, clergy, a variety of trades such as pewterers and printers, local amenities, property rights, industrial and agricultural practices, the economic, moral, and religious condition of the King's subjects: all were dealt with in bills which came under Parliament's scrutiny in the second half of Henry VIII's reign (1529–47). To some extent this deluge of private legislation might have been an accumulated backlog caused by the meeting of only one Parliament (1523) in the previous fourteen years (1515–29). Yet the input of individuals, local communities and occupations continued at the same high level in Edward VI's reign, despite an average of almost one session per year since 1529. It may well be that the reason for this is to be found in the new mantle of authority which clothed Parliament's actions as a result of its role in the 1530s, together with the less disciplined management of its activities after Cromwell's fall in 1540. It is impossible to tell.

What seems to be significant, however, is the increased activity of boroughs. They displayed a new assertiveness and more sophisticated lobbying techniques. London took the lead. It drafted its own legislative programmes [**doc. 24**], issued instructions to its members, made payments to the Commons' Speaker and other parliamentary officers, and actively canvassed for support. The fact that its bills so often failed was due to the fear, hostility, and opposition of smaller and less wealthy cities and towns (**110**). But they too, in their turn, were busy: York, Exeter, Norwich, and the Cinque Ports all promoted their own pet projects. The result of all this activity was a steady increase in the volume of private legislation. It proved to be a constant headache to those royal servants who acted as what we might now call 'conciliar managers', and whose responsibility was to ensure that their master or mistress obtained what he or she wanted from Parliament. Their first concern and duty was to guide official bills through relatively short, hectic sessions, but the timetable was under increasing pressure from the competing priorities of local, economic and individual interests. The net result was a rise in the number of abortive bills. That is not surprising. Some were not drafted properly, others were dashed by the efforts of rival interests, and many fell victim to sheer lack of time and the priority given to official measures. In Edward VI's reign, almost two-thirds of the bills before Parliament failed to pass, and most of those were privately promoted. In contrast, the legislative input shrank under Mary. This was partly a consequence of shorter and more contentious sessions, but above all of the formidable official programme presented in each Parliament. It does not alter or negate the fact that early Tudor parliaments were optimistic occasions, on which both the crown and a variety of prominent individuals and pressure groups hoped, indeed expected, to secure beneficial laws (**61**, pp. 55–6, 79–80, 82, 85–6, 106; **110**). In this respect Parliament was a public expression of paternal and patronal rule.

The productivity of parliaments

The deficiencies of the evidence (see pp. 24–5) make it impossible to chart accurately the record of productivity in the early Tudor parliaments. However, it is clear that even before the 1530s, when both Parliament and statute acquired a new authority, it was handling a considerable volume of legislative business. The seven parliaments (amounting to ten sessions) in Henry VII's reign passed 192 Acts, of which 120 were public (**38**, pp. 158–9). But numbers alone do not tell the whole story of legislative achievement. For example, some public Acts, pertaining to the entire realm, and usually of a social or economic nature, were sponsored by individual members. In contrast, others promoted by the crown were crucial to the country's political stability, without which any amount of well-meaning socio-economic legislation could not be effectively implemented. There was no significant change in the early years of Henry VIII's reign, when six sessions were held in six years, primarily to fund his military adventures: 121 Acts were passed, and the sessional output of statutes increased from nineteen to twenty. The disturbed Parliament of 1523, notable for Cardinal Wolsey's confrontation with the Commons over war-taxation, also produced thirty-five statutes. Admittedly most of them concerned individuals, localities, and sectional interests, whilst the tax grant – the purpose of its meeting – was disappointingly small. Nevertheless, as parliaments were occasions which benefited the community as well as the King, it was by no means unproductive; and Thomas Cromwell, a member of this Parliament, described (albeit with a cynical touch) the range of its activity [**doc. 15**].

When a new Parliament assembled in 1529, both royal and private expectations must have run high. The King was seeking a way out of his first marriage, whilst the fact that there had been just one Parliament in fourteen years (1515–29) probably produced a stockpile of private legislative proposals. Certainly the productivity level rose dramatically: 193 Acts were passed in the seven sessions of the Reformation Parliament (or a sessional average of between twenty-seven and twenty-eight) and 310 in the nine sessions between 1536 and 1547 (averaging between thirty-four and thirty-five). This was partly the consequence of a formidable government programme. Yet despite the fact that some of the official bills were contentious and/or complex, and undoubtedly time-consuming, private measures continued to claim a share of Parliament's time, energy and productivity: they amounted to almost one-third of the laws enacted between 1539 and 1547. In Edward VI's reign the parliamentary output continued at the same high level, despite conciliar divisions and even disarray. Successive aristocratic regimes pushed through a Protestant Reformation, together with a battery of laws dealing with law and order and a variety of social and economic matters. But at the same time legislative activity on the part of private interests showed no signs of abatement. The Marian record, however, stands in stark contrast to the parliamentary productivity of preceding Tudor reigns. The output of Mary's parliaments shrank to a mere eighteen or nineteen Acts in each session, and private bills were the chief victims (see p. 47).

Any assessment of productivity between 1485 and 1558 must take into account not only those bills which passed into law, but also those which failed. These cannot be measured with anything like precision before 1547, from which date the business records of both Houses survive. And even then, they do not record the bills which were handed into Parliament but which never reached the floor of Lords or Commons. Yet there is evidence enough to indicate that, even before 1547, many bills, mostly those of private origin, were abortive. They were usually the victims of hostile interests or, more especially, sheer lack of time. This impression is reinforced by the kind of precise analysis which is possible for the Edwardian and Marian parliaments. Only 166 of 453 bills read (or 35 per cent) eventually passed into law under Edward VI, and even less (32 per cent) under Mary, and few of the failures were of official origin. The figures provide another example of declining Marian productivity; so does the shrinking input of bills, down from a sessional Edwardian average of ninety-five to a mere forty-eight in the next reign. By any quantitative measure, Marian parliaments were relatively unproductive. However, numerical yardsticks can be misleading. Time and again Tudor governments which failed in initial attempts to pass measures into law, persisted and eventually succeeded. Henry VIII did this with the Statute of Uses, and Mary with laws to prosecute heretics and bring her husband under the protection of treason legislation. In the end, the crown almost always got what it wanted. The usual losers were the promoters of private bills. Yet repeated failure never succeeded in dousing their seemingly eternal optimism.

The legislative roles of the Lords and Commons

The incidence of bills originating in the two Houses provides a crude but useful measure of their respective legislative roles. It was the House of origin which licked a bill into shape, scrutinising, amending, even redrafting it, refining its language and engrossing (rewriting) it on parchment. Furthermore, as both official and private promoters were free to decide in which House to place their bills first, the relative popularity of Lords and Commons can be revealing about the public perception of them. Was one House more efficient and/or influential than the other? And given that a measure endorsed with the assent of one chamber was likely (though not certain) to pass the other, it was politically sensible for promoters to decide where opposition (if any) might manifest itself and so place the bill first in the other House. The idea was to give a measure some momentum before it encountered resistance. This is only a rough yardstick, because such bills were sometimes drastically amended, redrafted, or even rejected in the second chamber. In contrast, most grace bills (written on parchment and bearing the sign manual), attainders, restitutions, and general pardons, had an uncontested parliamentary passage. As these were conventionally placed in the Lords first, they must be discounted if the assessment of its initiating role is to be a realistic one. Furthermore, the amount and rates of lay taxation – often the very reason why Parliament was summoned – were invariably determined by the Commons. And most bills promoted by local, sectional, and economic interests were handed in there by their elected representatives as a matter of course. It might be assumed, therefore, that, as the Lower House was fully integrated into Parliament as a co-equal chamber, it also became the centre of parliamentary gravity and activity. However, this would be a simplistic and, at times, wildly inaccurate conclusion. Instead, the relative importance of the two Houses in parliamentary legislation fluctuated in accordance with current political conditions and other factors.

Although very little is known about Henry VII's parliaments, it looks as if both Lords and Commons were active in the law-making process. In contrast, the Lower House seems to have held centre-stage in the early years of his son's reign (1510–15 and 1523). That is hardly surprising. Parliaments were called to fund Henry VIII's wars. Furthermore the Commons was foremost in the counter-attack against the first Tudor's financial practices, and in the lay assault on ecclesiastical privileges and malpractices (see pp. 63–6). Yet the proportion of Acts commencing there could fall as low as 32 per cent in 1514. In other words, there was no general drift of legislative initiative to the Commons. Its 'arrival' as a full parliamentary partner did not diminish the Lords' role, but simply altered it. There was, perhaps, a more obvious trend in the Reformation Parliament (1529–36). The crown chose to introduce much of its legislative programme into the Lower House first, before it came up against the possible resistance of the lords spiritual. As a consequence, the Commons' share was 103 (or 53 per cent) of the output of 193 Acts. Yet between 1536 and 1553 the Lords took over as the chief initiator of successful bills: 59 per cent under Henry VIII and 64 per cent under Edward VI. Equally significant, from 1547, when the Commons' Journal permits such comparative measurements, is the proportion of *all* measures placed first in the Upper or Lower House, and the incidence of failure. Whereas only 41 per cent of bills began their parliamentary passage in the Edwardian Lords and 26 percent under Mary, almost three-fifths of them passed into law during the two reigns. In contrast the Commons' ratio of failure to success was 3:1 (**60**, pp. 175–6, 228–9). These figures, however, disguise a dramatic decline in the performance of the Marian Lords. Its share of initiated bills and Acts shrank – the latter down to 36 per cent. It was fractious and divided, with a smaller attendance but a greater inclination to reject outright both private and official measures.

Nevertheless, throughout the early Tudor period the House of Lords enjoyed impressive assets which were denied the Commons. The legal assistants – judges, the crown's legal counsel (Attorney- and Solicitor-General), serjeants-at-law, and the Master of the Rolls – provided an unmatchable pool of legal expertise and experience. They were there to advise the House on points of law, especially in the case of bills touching the prerogative or commonweal. The House leant heavily on their skills in the drafting, revision and amendment of bills, and frequently appointed them to committees, and to joint conferences with the Commons [**doc. 18**]. Some of the legal assistants (though not the judges) were employed in more mechanical and routine tasks: for example, engrossments and the conveyance of bills and messages to the Nether House.

Although lawyers were frequently elected to the Commons, their interests were often parochial. Moreover, if their careers prospered, especially in royal service, they often moved upwards to become legal assistants or nobles. Furthermore, the Lords was small (especially after the disappearance of the regulars in 1539–40) and of manageable size, whereas the Commons was large, steadily growing, and increasingly unwieldy. Unless they incurred royal displeasure or became involved in treason, bishops and peers were there for life, whilst some newly-ennobled recruits brought with them experience of the other House. As the older chamber, the Lord's procedures were tried and tested by time. If those of the Commons underwent a more rapid development in the sixteenth century, that was simply because it had to make up considerable leeway. At the same time, a process of procedural cross-fertilisation further refined and improved the legislative practices of both chambers.

There were other, more subtle and social advantages enjoyed by the Lords in its dealings with the Lower House. It was an assembly of the elite in Church and State and their social superiority, often intimidating at close contact, was carried over into Parliament. This was particularly evident in joint conferences, when the knights and burgesses stood bareheaded whilst their lordships remained seated and covered [**doc. 16**]. Impressive delegations from the Lords would sweep down to inform, declare, and cajole the Commons into action about the King's causes. Imperious messages instructed its members to 'order' the behaviour of their servants (1554) or to bring their business to a rapid conclusion in view of an impending dissolution of Parliament (1552). In such ways the muscle of social superiority was unsleeved from its normal discreet garb of parliamentary protocol. And usually it produced prompt action from a dutiful Commons. This was exemplified in the Lords' tax initiatives – as in 1512 and 1515 when the Lords informed the Commons of the reason for Parliament's summons; and in 1532, when Lord Chancellor More, at the head of a Lords' delegation, urged the Lower House to grant 'some reasonable aid' in order to prevent Scottish incursions. In Mary I's last Parliament (1558), the Lords went further and

encroached substantially on the Commons' customary right to initiate lay taxation and to determine the rate and amount [**doc. 17**].
Such interventions seem to have met with no hostile response. The
reason may have been that the nobles were usually patrons, many
of whose clients and kin were returned to the Lower House, often
with their assistance. The social homogeneity of the two chambers,
reinforced by the network of patron-client connections, encouraged
a co-operative relationship and diminished the possibility of inter-
cameral conflict.

Nevertheless political circumstances could diminish the legislative
importance of the early Tudor Lords. Parliaments which met in wartime automatically enhanced the Commons' role as the initiator of
subsidies, as was shown in 1510–15, 1523, 1542–5, 1547–50 and
1558. On the other hand, as demonstrated above, the Lords could
exert a formidable influence even on sensitive matters of the purse.
More important triggers of change were the placement of the
monarch's chief minister and parliamentary manager, and, above
all, the conduct of the two Houses. If, for example, opposition to
a particular official policy or bill was likely to occur in the Lords,
then it was a sound parliamentary tactic for the government to ally
with the other House and place its bills there first. Henry VIII did
this in the Reformation Parliament, at first because he feared the
opposition of the spiritual lords and then, increasingly, because
Thomas Cromwell, who sat in the Commons, managed his parliamentary affairs. However, in 1539–40 the newly-ennobled
Cromwell took his seat in the Lords, and immediately the upper
chamber became the more important one, where most official business was initiated. After Cromwell's fall in 1540, his successors
as Henry's chief advisers also sat there; and the aristocratic regimes
of Edward VI's reign strengthened the close ties between the House
of Lords and the crown. Therefore, between 1539 and 1553 the
Lords was unquestionably the more important House and the
dynamic element in the bicameral Parliament. However, in
the opening years of Mary I's reign (1553–5), the Lords betrayed
her trust in it. Court faction politics spilled over into the Upper
House, frustrating some of her objectives, and causing a downward
spiral in both its efficiency and its reputation as a responsible assembly (see pp. 72–5). The number of bills placed there first, and
its volume of business, shrank. Nor, despite its more loyal and
less fractious conduct in 1555 and 1558, had it recovered lost ground
by the time of Mary's death. Yet such changes tended to be tem-
porary, and they could be reversed rapidly by shifting political cir-

cumstances. So when William Cecil, Elizabeth I's chief minister, was elevated to the peerage as Lord Burghley in 1571, the centre of parliamentary gravity swung back to the House of Lords once more.

The managerial role of royal servants

There was nothing sinister in the crown's management of parliaments. They were called to service royal government. Therefore it was sensible, indeed responsible, to make such preparations as were necessary to ensure that their business was transacted smoothly, with a minimum of fuss (**56**, pp. 290–307). In practice that task was delegated to members of the King's Council and, after the emergence of the much smaller, tightly-knit, organised Privy Council in the 1530s, to Privy Councillors. Much of their work was accomplished before Parliament actually met. A business programme was devised and official bills were drafted. Major pieces of legislation might be drawn up by the monarch's chief advisers – for example, Thomas Cromwell in the 1530s – but frequently the services of the judges, Attorney- and Solicitor-General, all of whom assisted the Lords during parliamentary sessions, were enlisted [**docs 18, 19**]. Managerial activity also extended to elections to the Commons. This was not because it was (or was considered to be) the more troublesome House, but rather because its size and inefficiency and the volume of private legislation submitted to it threatened the passage of official bills. Managers were concerned to secure the election of a kind of government 'front-bench' of Councillors, and a supportive network of bureaucrats and household officials, together with loyal gentlemen and townsmen, especially lawyers – often described as the Council's men-of-business. To some extent this was achieved through the relatively few parliamentary boroughs controlled by the crown and by the discreet use of its patronage in others. Elsewhere, however, the process was primarily a social one. The local prestige of those who had royal favour could ensure their return to Parliament. Magnates who enjoyed borough influence, even to the extent of nominating one or both burgesses, might place their electoral patronage at the crown's disposal. And in the shires, where elections were not usually amenable to royal or noble direction, the freeholders with the franchise might nonetheless follow the lead and respect the wishes of the county's pre-eminent family. In other words, a modicum of royal activity was supplemented by the operation of powerful social forces working in the crown's favour.

Sometimes, however, especially in times of crisis, influence might give way to direct and overt intervention. In 1536 Cromwell ordered Canterbury to cancel its free election and choose instead two royal nominees; and the Duke of Northumberland had the audacity to instruct sheriffs that candidates recommended by Privy Councillors should be elected to the Parliament of March 1553 [**doc. 10**]. Such blatant intervention in the electoral process had, however, little, if any, chance of success. No greater fortune attended the issue of circular letters, which recommended that members should be men 'of knowledge and experience', or (as in Mary's reign) 'of the wise, grave and Catholic sort' [**doc. 20**]. They fell on the deaf ears of electors who, more often than not, acted out of respect and deference to familiar social superiors rather than in response to political pressures. In contrast, the House of Lords had a known and designated membership. Here the chief managerial concern was to ensure an adequate presence for the efficient transaction of business. Once again the first signs of systematic monitoring can be traced to Thomas Cromwell, who sometimes refused requests for absence, in the King's name (see p. 36).

Once Parliament had assembled, the conciliar managers and their aides had two ongoing responsibilities: to attend regularly, and to direct business in the royal interest, both on the floors of the two Houses and especially in committees. This could not be done by coercion or intimidation. Attempts to do so were counterproductive, as Wolsey discovered in 1523 (see pp. 40, 65). Success could be achieved only by guidance and persuasion. This was particularly so in the Commons, because many of its large membership were bound to be parliamentary novices in search of leadership. It was up to the Councillors sitting there to acquire the confidence of the House and to satisfy that need.

The Commons' Speaker was a vital figure in the managerial team. He was, in theory, the free choice of the House. However, in practice he was, and had been for much of the fifteenth century, a royal servant. From the beginning of Edward IV's reign one of the King's Councillors frequently filled the post: for example, Sir John Say (1463–5, 1467–8); William Catesby in Richard III's only Parliament (1484); Sir Thomas Lovel (1485–6), Richard Empson (1491–2) and Edmund Dudley (1504) under Henry VII. Most of the speakers in Henry VIII's early assemblies, including Sir Thomas More in 1523, were also royal Councillors. Other Councillors or prominent royal servants, such as Sir Thomas Audley (1529), Sir Richard Rich (1536), and Sir John Baker (1545 and 1547), presided in most of the remaining Henrician parliaments. In the following reigns the

Speakers were less prominent, but still identifiably connected with the crown (**43**, Chapters 5, 10–12). From 1461 they were substantially rewarded by the King for their parliamentary services. And gradually, as the managerial value of a trusty Speaker was recognised, the crown came to influence and even determine his selection. In this way, the Commons' right was transformed into a formality, as it elected the royal nominee at the opening of each Parliament. During the session the Speaker arranged the order of business. This enabled him to give priority to official measures, push private business into second place, regulate debate, and defer matters which might prove contentious or embarrassing to the Council. The Commons' seating arrangements gave the game away. Everyone 'sat as he came', except for the Councillors, who occupied the seats around the Speaker's chair. This enabled them to whisper instructions and advice to him on the direction of the Commons' affairs.

The Speaker's equivalent in the Lords was the Lord Chancellor, the first officer of state. He fulfilled a number of important parliamentary functions. With his Chancery clerks he activated a new Parliament by issuing writs which summoned individual lords spiritual and temporal and instructed sheriffs to arrange elections for the Commons. During the session he was the 'voyce and orator' of the sovereign (especially at the opening and closing ceremonies of Parliament), the mouthpiece and presiding officer of the Upper House, and the broker who conveyed requests or instructions between both the King and the Lords and the two chambers.

As a last resort, the monarch could intervene with the immense weight of his prestige and authority. Some forms of royal intervention came to an end under the early Tudors: for example, insertions and additions to bills after they had passed both Houses ended with Henry VII (**97**, p. 57), whilst his son was the last monarch to make royal appearances in both Houses. Nevertheless, apart from the minor Edward VI, the Tudors remained active behind the scenes: consulting their parliamentary managers, issuing them with instructions, and despatching messages to the two Houses. At the end of each session they emerged to exercise the prerogative of assent or veto to bills which had passed Lords and Commons. Henry VIII in particular became a master of the managerial arts. He was always available to parliamentary delegations, to whom he could be affable or intimidating, and always impressive [**doc. 21**]. And when, in 1553, Mary I dismissed a parliamentary petition against her proposed marriage to Philip of Spain, her imperious manner was reminiscent of her father [**doc. 29**] – although, apart from that, she was a failure as a manager. In any case, even the monarch could not force parliaments into unpopular courses. The recipe for success was the Councillors' ability to persuade the two Houses into willing acquiescence. This in turn could be achieved only by a general parliamentary consensus. If it was not forthcoming, they worked for some kind of compromise. Of this there is no better example than the way in which the Edwardian Privy Council allayed local concern and defused Commons' opposition to the bill dissolving the chantries in 1547 [**doc. 22**].

There was no effective substitute for a combination of tact, persistence, and an understanding of parliamentary interests and susceptibilities. However, this notion was unfamiliar to Charles V, head of the House of Habsburg, Holy Roman Emperor, King of Spain, and father of Mary I's consort, Philip. He was used to handling the parliaments (*Cortes*) of his Spanish kingdom with a cynical mixture of commands and financial carrots. Therefore, in order to forestall possible parliamentary opposition to the marriage between his son and England's Queen, he distributed through Simon Renard, his ambassador at her Court, a profusion of gifts and promises of future preferment. The recipients were prominent nobles, bishops and other men who might be influential in Parliament. Thus between 1553 and 1555 the normal managerial arts of persuasion were supplemented by financial inducements [**doc. 23**] – but all to little effect (see pp. 73–5).

The most important ingredient of a successful Parliament, so far as the crown was concerned, was the ability of its managerial co-ordinator and chief. So important was his role that the centre of parliamentary initiative shifted from one House to another in accordance with his placement. Nothing is known about Henry VII's managers, or even who they were. Thereafter the quality of the crown's managers varied. Cardinal Wolsey's autocratic temper and arrogance were unsuited to the task. The result was mutual distrust and dislike. In contrast, the palm for managerial excellence must go to Thomas Cromwell in the 1530s. But the collective management which operated between Cromwell's fall and Henry VIII's death (1540–7) was divided and weakened by aristocratic ambition, anticlericalism and religious conflict. The quality did not improve thereafter. Somerset (1547–9), another autocrat, was incompetent and out of touch with political realities. His successor, Northumberland, was ineffectual, lazy, and unsure. Mary's first Lord Chancellor, Bishop Gardiner, was a self-assured parliamentary manager and capable of generating personal loyalty in some of those around him; but he was also self-opinionated and dogmatic. The proud prelate incurred noble hostility, divided Court and Council, and caused faction politics to spill over into Parliament. It was only with William Cecil, Elizabeth I's chief adviser, that management was restored to a Cromwellian level of quality.

6 The Politics of Early Tudor Parliaments

The nature and purpose of parliamentary politicking

Revisionist studies of early modern English parliamentary history have corrected some of the earlier misconceptions about the institution and, at the same time, enlarged our knowledge of it. However, there is now the danger of a new distortion: that the great issues, disagreements, even conflicts, which undoubtedly figured in that history, will be understated, ignored, or swept under the carpet. The revisionists' predecessors treated Parliament as a political institution. The revisionists themselves emphasise that it was a place of business. But one should not exclude the other – rather we should understand that it accommodated both. There is a simple reason for this. For all participating parties the end and purpose of a Parliament was the enactment of bills into law. Ideally, this was when royal needs were met, urgent affairs of the realm were dealt with, and at least some private aspirations were satisfied. In all of these ways, Parliament was a place of business. At the same time, politicking was the natural means of getting things done and, sometimes, of frustrating them. In this sense, parliaments were very political occasions, during which political skills were the prerequisite of success.

This was true not only of urgent royal necessities, such as additional funding, incorporated in subsidy bills, or the resolution of great affairs, especially during the Reformation. It was equally applicable to the advancement or defeat of small causes. They might concern the projects of localities and economic interests, especially those of London (**110**); the statutory endorsement of marriage settlements and property deals; the restitution of traitors' heirs; the transference of local feuds into the two Houses of Parliament [**doc. 24**]; or a parliamentary extension of the competition between ambitious politicians or overmighty nobles [**doc. 9**]. In pursuit of their various ends, bill-promoters became parliamentary politicians. They lobbied members, Councillors and the Commons' Speaker for support. They canvassed for votes, employed 'fee'd'* (paid) knights and burgesses to speak on their behalf, and applied to patrons for assistance. They used persuasive speech in debate and strove to advance or block measures in bill committees. If the promoters were fortunate enough to enjoy royal favour, they were sometimes able to secure the sign manual on their bills. Sophisticated political skills, of the kind we associate with modern parliamentary politics, were already well-developed by the time Elizabeth I became Queen.

Such techniques were employed by opponents as well as promoters of bills and this was equally true of measures designed to deal with private and great public causes. However, successful delaying tactics and, even more, overt opposition, were both disruptive and wasteful of time. They were threats to the managerial ideals of consensus and parliamentary productivity. Therefore the skilful politicking of conciliar managers was crucial to the success of early Tudor parliaments. If success was not always achieved, that was sometimes the result of unpopular royal policies. Whatever produced a disturbed Parliament, however, some responsibility for the failure to fulfil royal goals always rested with the managerial chief. And the parliamentary consequences were even worse when, as happened in Mary I's reign, even the Privy Councillors reneged on their duty (see pp. 72–5). In this case, politicking in Court and Council produced parliamentary conflict. Normally, however, political activity was not synonymous with division and conflict. Indeed, constructive and responsible politicking was an essential ingredient in the attainment of fruitful parliaments.

Co-operation and conflict: the pre-Reformation parliaments, 1485–1523

Little is known about parliamentary politicking in Henry VII's reign. Perhaps it is for this reason, or simply because the King was in firm control, that occasions of sharp disagreement or opposition to royal actions and policies are rarely recorded. The two known instances chiefly concerned property rights, hardly surprising in a bicameral Parliament of propertied men. Although the many attainders by which Henry VII attempted to proscribe the Yorkist leadership passed into law, they came in for a good deal of criticism from Commons' members in 1485. Parliamentary attainders involved the forfeiture of the guilty persons' property, and this may have been viewed with concern as a general threat to property rights (**38**, pp. 50–60, 114). Whatever the reason, attainder 'sore was questioned with' and 'there was many gentlemen against it' [**docs 25, 26**]. Secondly, in the Parliament of 1504, Henry VII's request for feudal aids [**doc. 13**] would have necessitated an investigation into the feudal obligations of property owners. This prospect caused widespread consternation at a time when many of them were attempting to conceal or evade their dues (**38**, pp. 52, 56–7).

These isolated episodes must be kept in perspective. On the one hand, it is clear from the earliest surviving parliamentary diary, kept by the Colchester members in 1485, that vigorous debate and sharp disagreements were already characteristics of Commons' proceedings [**doc. 26**]. But such characteristics did not necessarily imply criticism of royal government, and should not be misconstrued as such. The sparse evidence of Henry's parliaments suggests that co-operation and productivity typified them. In any case the Commons' freedom to speak on matters relating to the crown was strictly limited, whilst the presence of Councillors, who could report to Henry on members' conduct, must have been inhibiting. Furthermore, Parliament's venue was royal Westminster, where the panoply and ceremonial must have reinforced the natural deference accorded to the King. The decisive political force in parliaments was identified by a member in 1485. Despite opposition to the many attainders, he wrote that 'it would not be, for it was the King's pleasure'.

The early parliaments of Henry VIII (1510–23) differed significantly. Firstly, much more is known about them – and particularly about their politics. Secondly, war-taxation, as the chief cause of their meeting, thrust the Commons into prominence. Thirdly, the emergence of an autocratic minister, monopolising authority under the King in a way unknown in Henry VII's reign, created problems in relations between Commons, Lords, and the royal authority delegated and embodied in the person of Cardinal Wolsey. The fact that he was a member of the clergy sharpened the edge of popular anti-clericalism, whilst his accumulation of power antagonised great men such as the Dukes of Norfolk and Suffolk, whose influence had diminished as a consequence. Certainly there is evidence of increasing criticism of royal government, and of disagreements between the three members of the parliamentary trinity. However, an examination of the nature and motivation of the disputes which occurred reveals that they were not parliamentary confrontations with the monarch. In 1510 the Commons took the lead in legislation which was designed to prevent a repetition of the punitive financial practices (even malpractices) of Henry VII's government. It was the new King, however, who gave the signal for such action, when he arrested his father's chief and unpopular agents, Richard Empson and Edmund Dudley. Indeed, he allowed, even encouraged, the reform movement. It produced some hard bargaining and even disagreement on terms, but there was no confrontation. The Lords acted as a broker, carefully balancing the royal prerogative and the subject's rights. And, once again, the process was characterised by co-operation rather than conflict. Moreover, Henry VIII made it clear that statutory reform would not be allowed to diminish in any way the rates of customs duties which his father had levied (**55**, pp. 35–6). The 'reform campaign' of 1510 was little more than a public-relations exercise in which the King retained the whip-hand.

In 1515 there occurred a crisis of major proportions. It can be traced back directly to the Act which, three years earlier, had limited 'benefit of clergy' to the priesthood. Previously, by a gradual process of enlargement over centuries, the privilege had extended to anyone who was technically in holy orders and literate enough to read aloud a verse of the first psalm. Such persons, charged with common-law offences which were punishable by death, only had to read the 'neck verse' for their cases to be transferred from the King's courts to those of the Church. If they were convicted there, they escaped with a light penalty. This was offensive to the anti-clerical laity, to the secular courts, and to the crown, which sought to close this loophole in its system of justice. However, whilst the 1512 Act prevented abuse of 'benefit' by literate laymen, it left clerical privilege intact. And when Parliament met in 1515 this had become a hot political issue because of the Hunne case (**75**).

Richard Hunne, a London merchant, fell foul of the ecclesiastical authorities over the payment of a customary fee to the local priest for burying his infant son. When a church court found against Hunne, whose refusal to pay could not be justified in law, he responded with a writ of *praemunire* in one of the King's courts. Praemunire was a deadly weapon. It could be employed against any 'invasion of the King's regality' (which included the jurisdiction of his courts) and the penalties extended to loss of goods and indefinite imprisonment. Bishop Fitzjames of London, an arch-reactionary, had Hunne incarcerated in his prison on a charge of heresy; and there, in December 1514, he was found hanging by his neck in his cell. The official ecclesiastical verdict was suicide, but public opinion cried 'murder'. Bishop Fitzjames' insistence that, as clergy, the prison officials implicated in Hunne's death were immune from actions in the King's courts raised the political temperature as Parliament met. The resolution of these issues during, and between, the two sessions of 1515 was a complex process and need not be recounted in detail here (**55**, pp. 51–8). However, the issues involved, their impact on Parliament, and their significance for the future are of some importance, especially as the Act of 1512 was of limited duration and due for renewal. The lords spiritual in the Upper House blocked its re-enactment and those suspected of murder escaped the law. In the short term, the Church won. Although Cardinal Wolsey was obliged to seek pardon for the clergy from Henry VIII, and did so in the presence of the Lords and Commons (an indignity which would not have warmed him to parliaments), clerical immunity remained untouched.

Nevertheless the whole episode had raised important matters of principle about Church-State relations, and the borderline of authority between them. On the other hand, this was not a dress-rehearsal for the 1530s, when King-in-Parliament severed relations with the papacy and asserted the State's supremacy over the Church. It would require the example of the European Reformation and, above all, the King's 'great matter' to achieve that. Mere anti-clerical prejudice, as expressed in 1515, could not. However, the parliamentary alignments are significant. During the proceedings on this matter in the two sessions of 1515, there was no confrontation between King and Commons, nor between the two Houses. Instead, there was a secular coalition – the King siding with the peers, Commons, and anti-clerical prejudice – against a beleagured clergy and its parliamentary spokesmen, the lords spiritual [**doc. 25**].

Eight years passed before Cardinal Wolsey, whose autocratic and clerical distaste for the parliamentary way of doing things must have been reinforced by the events of 1515, was obliged to call another Parliament. When it met, the Commons proved unsympathetic to Wolsey's request for war revenue. Coming hard on top of the loan of 1522–3, he was demanding a subsidy levied at the unprecedented rate of 4s (20p) in the pound (see p. 40). His personal descent on the Lower House, decked out in all his finery and with an imposing retinue, was hardly guaranteed to endear him to members who were more concerned with the kingdom's poverty. One complained about the drain on money and men in order to acquire useless bits of territory in France. If there was implicit in this gibe a criticism of the wasteful and futile foreign policy of Wolsey's royal master, Parliament's proceedings remained essentially a confrontation between the cardinal and the Commons [**doc. 25**]. Yet there may be

more to it than that. When Wolsey informed the Lower House that
the Lords had already granted the rate requested, the Upper House
denied his claim and left him isolated. Were his enemies, the Dukes
of Norfolk and Suffolk and other disgruntled nobles, seeking to em-
barrass him? After all, Wolsey's fall in 1529 (and Cromwell's demise
in 1540) were both assisted, if not actually engineered, by great magnates. The question can only be posed; it cannot be answered (**46**,
pp. 116–22; **55**, pp. 88–92).

Conflict and co-operation: the Reformation parliaments to 1553

The radical and rapid changes of the 1530s altered the English State
and Church, and English society itself, in many ways. Any upheaval
of such dimensions inevitably produces a crop of victims and this
was no exception: some lost their lives, others their freedom,
authority, rights or privileges, property or livelihoods. Such drastic
restructuring did not proceed without opposition. And, as Parliament was the mechanism which, in response to royal initiatives, effected the changes, resistance was bound to surface there. The roots
of that resistance, however, were many and varied. The most obvious and identifiable group, designated by G. R. Elton as the
'Aragonese faction', were principally supporters of Henry's first
wife, Catherine of Aragon, and opponents of the annulment of his
marriage to her. But its members and adherents were also concerned about the wider implications of Henry VIII's actions.
Therefore they included defenders of clerical privilege and papal
supremacy. Furthermore, it was a dangerous network because it
included men in high and influential positions. Thomas More's
links with it were those of an informant rather than a political ac-
tivist (**55**, pp. 116–7; **57**, pp. 117–9; **63**, pp. 138–42), but the more
committed members included Eustace Chapuys (the ambassador of
Catherine's nephew, Charles V), the Queen's chaplains, devout
Catholic nobles and gentlemen, and prominent ecclesiastics like
Bishop Fisher of Rochester. Its parliamentary network was particularly strong in the Upper House, with its majority of spiritual
lords, but it had adherents and voices in the Commons too. The
Aragonese faction could also count on the conservative instincts of
other members to support it on particular issues. For example, the
bill to deprive the Pope of his customary right to annates (payments
due to him from newly-appointed bishops and abbots) met stiff opposition in both Houses in 1532. The King had to attend the

Lords frequently, and even make a rare appearance in the Commons in order to secure its passage – and even then only with significant modification to its original terms.

The most important corporate body opposed to Henry VIII's move towards schism, as the drastic solution to his marital problems, was the Church. However, the spiritual lords in the Upper House were isolated and under siege. So too were the bishops and lower clergy in the Convocations (assemblies) of Canterbury and York, the former of which met concurrently with Parliament. The clergy's role in royal service, and therefore their value to the King, was declining as an educated laity displaced them in government. They were on the defensive against an anti-clerical prejudice which had been honed on the recent Hunne case [**docs. 25, 27**]. The way in which Parliament persecuted, and attempted to prosecute, the fallen and helpless Wolsey in 1529 was simply a portent of the clergy's fate in the 1530s. Indeed, they became the chief victims of the schism. Their immunities and authority were stripped away, and they were subordinated to a new head who was a resident, omnipresent, harsh royal taskmaster. The clergy's brief resistance in Lords and Convocation ended in ignominious capitulation in 1531–2 [**doc. 27**]. Thereafter it was weak, ineffectual, and increasingly divided. The disappearance of the regulars reduced the lords spiritual to a permanent minority in the Lords, despite the creation of six new sees in 1540–2. And these survivors could not present a united front, because the infiltration of Protestantism split the episcopal bench asunder. Stephen Gardiner (Winchester), John Stokesley (Lincoln) and other conservatives were confronted not only by Thomas Cranmer, Henry's choice as Archbishop of Canterbury, but also by reforming bishops advanced by Cromwell: Nicholas Shaxton (Salisbury), Hugh Latimer (Worcester) and Edward Fox (Hereford). After 1533 the episcopate was divided and demoralised.

The ideological politics of religion merged with new sources of conflict provoked by the changes of the 1530s. There was the hostility of the old nobility towards the new men, especially Cromwell who, like Wolsey, had displaced them from their customary prominence in the King's counsels. There was the promotion (and sometimes destruction) of the kin of Henry's Queens: Boleyns, Seymours and Parrs, victors or victims of Henrician marital politics. And there was the eternal competition among ambitious politicians for royal favour and advancement. The end result was continuous, often bitter faction conflict in both Court and Council. Moreover, it intensified in the early 1540s, when it became clear that Henry would die before his son came of age. Thus far it would seem that factions were concerned with personal advancement, not principles and policies. To a great extent this is true, although religious differences did introduce an ideological element into faction alignments: so the Duke of Norfolk and Bishop Gardiner headed a conservative grouping, whilst the Seymour interest leant towards reform. However, the bedrock of the faction was neither political nor religious but social. Its core was a kinship connexion, enlarged by the patron-client bond, territorial affiliations and business associations. It lacked organisation, discipline and permanence, whilst its size and membership depended on the fortunes of its aristocratic head. Nevertheless, at the centre of Tudor government, factions did engage in political activities.

It was unfortunate for Thomas Cromwell that, whilst many men looked to him as the King's chief minister for favours, he did not create a faction around him. In 1539, Henry VIII, after several years of mild flirtation with the reformed religion which Cromwell patronised, reverted to a hard-line Catholic position with the Act of six articles. This laid down a corpus of Catholic dogma, together with harsh penalties for nonconformity. When the measure was introduced, Cromwell was taken by surprise and his arch-enemy, Norfolk, steered it through the Lords. This exposed the minister's dangerously isolated position. He had guided his royal master into a distasteful marriage with Anne of Cleves. Norfolk and Gardiner seized their opportunity and convinced a susceptible king that Cromwell had heretical leanings. In 1539 Parliament was used to defeat the detested upstart minister, and in 1540 to destroy him by Act of attainder, without a trial. In other words, factions resorted to parliaments to achieve their ends, but they did so in a discreet manner, embodying their victories in statutes which were couched in formal and legal language, with the occasional obsequious touch. To all appearances parliamentary harmony remained.

The same was true after Cromwell's fall, which was not a parliamentary milestone. Reforms begun before, in both the law and administration, continued afterwards. So did faction politics, with a conservative ascendancy until 1543/4, when the pendulum began to move towards the Seymours and others inclined to religious reform. Near the end of his reign, Henry excluded Gardiner from his Council, had Norfolk's son tried and executed, and had the Duke himself attainted by the Parliament which ended abruptly with Henry's own death in 1547. Divorces, annulments, statutory killings by attainder, unprecedented war-taxation, delegated legislative powers: there seemed to be nothing which the old, experienced King could not obtain with ease from loyal parliaments. However, that is not the whole story. In 1539 the bill which attempted to define the constitutional authority of proclamations and establish a statutory machinery for their enforcement, made its way into law only after extensive criticism in Parliament, which led to redrafting and substantial amendment (**55**, pp. 285–6).

More prolonged and productive of hostility was Henry's tenacious campaign to secure his feudal rights (**107**). Propertied families, whose lands were held by feudal tenure, were liable to pay dues to the crown when the head of the family died and his heir inherited. In order to avoid those burdensome, sometimes crippling, death duties, more and more landowners resorted to the 'use'. During his lifetime a landowner would divest himself of legal ownership of his property in favour of a body of trustees. They administered the estate on his behalf, but he continued to enjoy the profits thereof. On his death, they continued to perform the same function to the use not only of his heir, but of other beneficiaries named by him. The use solved two serious problems for the propertied classes. The common law did not recognise bequests of land by will, and so property descended to a landowner's heir, usually his eldest son (primogeniture). However, the use enabled him to reward friends, servants and other relatives as well. Secondly, individual trustees might die, but the trust (the 'feoffees to uses') did not, and so feudal dues were not owed to the King. When the Reformation Parliament met in 1529, after twenty years of expensive military and diplomatic activity, Henry sought to stage a financial recovery, and one of his targets was feudal dues. His action was justified and his demands moderate. He reached an agreement with the peers in Parliament, whereby he would be guaranteed just one-third of his legitimate entitlement. But, of course, this was not an Act of parliament. Three years later, a bill containing similar terms, and designed to secure the statutory approval of the Commons, ran into serious problems there. Understandably the King's patience wore thin. The death of Lord Dacre of the South in 1533 enabled him to provoke a test case. If Henry intimidated the judges in order to secure a favourable decision, it must be admitted that his cause was a just one. Their verdict invalidated not only Dacre's will, but all wills and uses [**doc. 28**]. In 1536 this enabled the King to obtain the Statute of Uses from the defenceless Lords and Commons. Under its terms, land could no longer be bequeathed by will; the use acquired legal recognition, but the 'beneficiary' (the landowner, who eventually died), not the body of trustees (which never died) was acknowledged as the legal owner, and therefore his estate was liable for all (not just one-third) of the feudal payments due to the King [**doc. 28**].

This amounted to a total victory for Henry. But it was too complete. The Statute of Uses was one of the causes of a serious rebellion, the Pilgrimage of Grace, in 1536. It failed, but compromise was necessary, and four years later Henry, astute and experienced politician that he was, recognised this. The Statute of Wills of 1540 acknowledged trusts as the owners, legitimised wills, and confined the application of feudal dues to one-third of the owner's lands. The prolonged issue, stretching over eleven years, typifies Henry's patience, parliamentary skills and ability to coerce the judges – and, above all, the need to search for consensus, and to reconcile the differing interests of crown and governing class with some kind of parliamentary compromise. Indeed, this is the abiding impression left by a study of the Henrician parliaments of 1529–47. Despite the many issues of fundamental importance placed before the two Houses by royal government, and despite the sharpening religious antagonism of the 1530s and 1540s, the essential parliamentary characteristics remained those of productivity and consensus. Even the intrusion of faction politics was, as we have seen, muted, discreet, and decently clothed in statutory garb.

This was not to be the case in Edward VI's reign. The parliamentary landscape changed, dramatically and overnight. There was no longer a powerful adult King, but a minor in tutelage to aristocratic governors; no longer a royal focus of loyalty but divisive aristocratic politics; no longer a discreet veil thrown over the competition of factions in parliaments, but the exposure of their naked conflicts for all to see. Furthermore, the House of Lords, where Edward's noble governors sat, along with their most prominent supporters, became the political focus of Parliament. The Protestant Reformation (moderate, even ambiguous, under Somerset; more radical and uncompromising under Northumberland) encountered its chief parliamentary obstacle there. The conservative bishops, led by Nicholas Heath (Worcester), Edmund Bonner (London), George Day (Chichester) and Cuthbert Tunstal (Durham) resisted every step of the way. Their deprivations wore down the Catholic resistance, especially since the government imprisoned its most formidable Catholic opponent, Bishop Gardiner, and eventually deprived him of his see [**doc. 30**]. Nevertheless, the Edwardian House of Lords was the battleground where the conservatives, afforced by Derby,

Dacre and a few other peers, fought a persistent rearguard action in each session against the Protestant battalions. However, few Catholic bishops remained to oppose the second Edwardian prayer book of 1552 (**60**, pp. 74–5, 89–91).

Under Edward VI, factions hunting for power experienced a greater freedom in the pursuit of their goals and the hounding of their rivals. The classic case was that of Protector Somerset's younger brother, Thomas Seymour. A barony and the office of Lord Admiral (which he misused and abused) could not quench the thirst of his ambition or assuage his jealousy of his brother. Seymour embarked on a brief, frenetic and reckless political career, which included plans to marry Princess Elizabeth, release Edward VI from Somerset's guardianship, and raise an army from money embezzled from the Bristol mint. In order to promote his ambitions, he turned to both Houses of Parliament for support in 1548–9 [**doc. 9**]. Instead he was attainted by Parliament in that session and duly executed. His high-minded brother failed to see that Thomas' death had been engineered by his own enemies, and that his refusal to spare him would blacken his own reputation. Kinship was an essential loyalty in early Tudor England. By the time Parliament reassembled in November 1549, the Protector himself had been toppled from power. Without the controlling hand and brooding presence of Henry VIII, faction politics had more overt parliamentary repercussions.

Nor was this confined to the ruling circles. A 'new' rising gentleman, Thomas Wharton, who was ennobled in 1544, feuded incessantly with old-established peers such as the Cliffords, Earls of Cumberland, and the Lords Dacre, in the far north-west of England [**doc. 24**]. As parliamentary management, discipline, and direction declined in the Edwardian parliaments, the Whartons and their opponents brought their county rivalries down with them to Westminster (**61**, pp. 95–6). Whether the antagonists were members of the ruling clique, like the Seymour brothers, or local magnates, such as the Whartons and Cliffords, they were ready to politick in both Houses. Whilst the Edwardian Lords was the political focus of Parliament, the enactment of new laws required the assent of both Houses. That is why both the impetuous Thomas Seymour and Cumberland's cool political agent, Thomas Jolye, canvassed support in Lords and Commons. Yet in spite of the rifts exposed and widened by Edwardian aristocratic misgovernment, the bicameral Parliament still mirrored a homogeneous governing elite of landed men, who were linked by patron-client connections, kinship, and other socio-economic bonds. In this respect at least, Edwardian parliaments did not differ from their Henrician predecessors.

The Marian experience, 1553–58

Five parliaments, the last of which met twice, were summoned during Mary's short reign. Indeed the first four sat within the very short space of twenty-six months. This frequency was due to her formidable legislative programme and to the parliamentary resistance which it encountered. It was a reactionary package which was of fundamental importance to both the crown and the propertied classes. In brief, Mary wished to reverse the religious changes of the last two reigns, by restoring Catholicism and papal supremacy, returning expropriated property to the Church, and reviving the laws against heresy. It was a programme which inevitably aroused fears and provoked opposition in many quarters: amongst old Henricians loyal to the King's memory, Edwardian Protestants, and all the possessors of ex-monastic and other Church lands. In addition there was the Queen's intention to marry Philip of Spain. If the Catholic restoration was to be permanent, she must have heirs of her body who could be raised in her faith. Otherwise, on her death the crown would pass to her Protestant half-sister Elizabeth. The proposed marriage stirred up English prejudices and hostility against foreigners, and provoked fears of Spanish Catholic intolerance and of the danger that the country would be dragged into the frequent Franco-Spanish wars.

Such anxieties and enmity were bound to surface in Parliament, where alone Mary could realise her ambitions. However, her personal determination and courage were counter-balanced by her political ineptitude. She appointed a large, unwieldy Privy Council, which was a bewildering mixture of restored Catholic bishops, old experienced Henrician civil servants, new nobles such as the Earl of Pembroke who had made their fortunes in the Edwardian Protestant regimes, and her own faithful household servants. This body was riven with conflicting personalities and factions, and therefore ill-equipped to manage parliaments in the royal interest. Most serious was the mutual antagonism of Stephen Gardiner and William Paget. Gardiner, the Henrician Bishop of Winchester who had been imprisoned and deprived for his opposition to the Edwardian Reformation, was now restored and appointed Lord Chancellor. He had been a loyal supporter of Henry's supremacy, but ambition, or his bitter Edwardian experiences, now made him the ardent advocate of Marian religious policies. In contrast, Paget was a secular politician, no doctrinaire in religion, an anti-clerical owner of expropriated Church property, and one who had prospered in Edward VI's reign. However, the factions forming around these men were impermanent and fluid, as Councillors switched allegiances on different issues. In any case the conciliar divisions were numerous and varied, and they did not simply polarise around the Gardiner-Paget struggle.

There were two important parliamentary consequences of the divisions within Court and Council. The first was the extension of faction politics into parliaments. This was not new. It had happened, albeit discreetly, in the later Henrician parliaments (see p. 68) and more overtly in Edward VI's reign (see pp. 70–1). But Marian factions, in pursuit of their opponents, were prepared even to sacrifice her interests and sabotage some of her most important measures. Secondly, as Gardiner, Paget, and many of the other prominent Councillors sat in the Lords, this House became an arena of conflict, with harmful effects on its customary efficiency, sense of responsibility, and productivity. Mary's first Parliament (1553) was a portent of what was to happen in 1554–5. The bill to reverse the Edwardian Reformation had to overcome stiff resistance in the Commons, which also rejected her attempt to restore the Bishopric of Durham, suppressed in the previous reign. Thus far the focus of opposition was the Lower House. In contrast, the concerted parliamentary campaign against Mary's marital plans was organised by her own Lord Chancellor. Gardiner opposed a foreign match and instead promoted the candidature of Edward Courtenay, Earl of Devon. Both feckless and a political nonentity, Courtenay nevertheless became a rallying-point for opponents of the Spanish marriage. Gardiner, an experienced parliamentary manager, brought together a number of disparate forces in the Earl's support: the Edwardian Pembroke, the stout Catholics Derby and Stourton, and Mary's own household servants [**doc. 29**]. To these he added what was called by contemporaries 'Winchester's faction', including some 15–25 Commons' members who owed their election to him [**doc. 30**]. However, the hopes of this coalition collapsed in November 1553 when Mary imperiously rejected a parliamentary petition which begged her to marry an Englishman. Gardiner promptly became an enthusiastic promoter of the Spanish Match [**doc. 29**].

Mary's initial parliamentary experience was to be repeated in her second and third assemblies, but with an important difference. In

1553 overt opposition had been Commons-centred. Noble and episcopal politicians had confined themselves to the less confrontational tactics of lobbying and petitioning (**60**, pp. 183–90; **61**, pp. 107–8, 113; **70**, pp. 74–90). That was all to change. Sir Thomas Wyatt's abortive anti-Spanish rebellion, early in 1554, ensured that there would be no serious resistance to the ratification of Mary's marriage in her second Parliament (April-May 1554). Furthermore the Bishopric of Durham was restored at the second attempt. But there was little else to comfort the Queen. This was because Gardiner had devised his own legislative programme dealing with heresy, papal supremacy, secularised lands, and Elizabeth's exclusion from the succession. Protestants, anti-clericals, opponents of the papacy, possessors of Church property, and Elizabeth's champions all found a focus of resistance in the Lords, where Paget and his leading supporters (as well as Gardiner) sat. Despite elaborate managerial preparations – the creation of new bishops and peers and the distribution of Habsburg patronage (see p. 59) – it was in the Upper House that conflict erupted. The bills against heresy were thrown out; Mary's attempt to protect her consort with the treason laws was rendered worthless by amendments in a Lord's committee [**doc. 31**]; and Gardiner dared not even raise the succession question. Conciliar factions had torpedoed the schemes of both the Lord Chancellor and the Queen (**60**, pp. 190–4; **61**, pp. 108–10; **70**, pp. 91–104).

When Parliament reassembled in November 1554, it was in the presence of Mary and her Spanish husband. It might be called a royal success. Papal supremacy was restored and the delay in its enactment was due to the obstinacy of the Pope's legate, Cardinal Pole. He was reluctant to issue a dispensation which would allow owners of secularised lands to remain in possession, and he yielded only after intensive and prolonged pressure (**70**, pp. 105–15). The heresy laws were also enacted, this time without much difficulty, and a chastened House of Lords now passed the bill to extend the protection of the treason laws to King Philip. However, the Commons enlarged the section dealing with arrangements for the government of the realm if Mary were to predecease her husband, leaving a minor heir. It was now provided that Philip, assisted by a regency council of peers, was to govern during the minority. The nobles, some of whom doubted Spanish intentions, were offended by arrangements sponsored in the Commons and on which they had not been consulted. During the bill's passage in December a number of peers and 106 Commons' members withdrew. The meaning and significance of this has been the subject of unresolved historical debate. Were members anxious to get home for a family Christmas, or did offended nobles, and their Commons' clients acting under instructions, make a silent gesture of protest with their feet (**60**, pp. 195–8; **61**, pp. 110–11; **70**, pp. 47–50, 119–21)? Whatever the motive for their departure, there was undoubted politicking behind the scenes. Thus, when the treason bill eventually passed into law, the offending section on the regency council had been dropped. Nevertheless, Mary had some cause to be satisfied with this Parliament. She had unburdened herself of the odious title of supreme head; heretics could now be burned, a prospect which no doubt gratified the vengeful Gardiner; and Philip's position was more secure. But it must have been a qualified satisfaction. Church lands were not restored, and Mary was compelled to recognise that parliamentary consent to her husband's coronation would not be forthcoming (**60**, pp. 195–7; **70**, pp. 105–27).

In the remaining parliaments of the reign the Lords reverted to its customary sober and responsible conduct. Doubtless the death of Gardiner, early in the 1555 Parliament, substantially reduced the heat of faction. Instead, it was the Commons which hotly contested Mary's attempt to restore first fruits and tenths to the Pope. Furthermore, by the audacious (and pre-rehearsed?) action of seizing the keys, locking the doors of the Commons' chamber, and calling for a snap vote, Sir Anthony Kingston and other dissidents secured the rejection of the bill to punish those who had gone into exile during Mary's reign. In her last Parliament (1558), which was called to fund the war with France, into which England had been dragged by Philip, the Lords was prominent in the drafting of the subsidy bill (see p. 55). This showed that it had resumed its old role as the crown's reliable mainstay. Yet the return to former ways could not erase from the memory the manner in which it had let the Queen down so badly in 1553–4.

Her reign was marked and marred by parliaments which were more disturbed than at any other time during the English Reformation. More often than not (apart from 1555) the Lords proved to be Mary's stumbling-block. And, though the evidence is largely circumstantial, it is sufficient to suggest that some of the Commons' hostile actions were stage-managed, or at least prompted, by patrons in the Upper House. It is important to recall once more that the two chambers consisted of men from one homogeneous governing class. They were part of a latticework of socio-economic and political relationships. The fact that between a quarter and a third of the

House of Commons were kin, friends or clients of great men in the Lords, and therefore in a subordinate, deferential role, simply mirrored the social realities of the world beyond Westminster. It would be unrealistic to suppose that such relationships, and accompanying obligations, were suspended during parliamentary sessions. However, the Marian House of Lords overstepped the mark. Instead of using their adherents in the Commons as their front-line troops, aristocratic and episcopal patrons were instrumental in sinking some of the measures launched by the Queen. In doing so they forfeited not only her good opinion but that of the sponsors of private bills. So the legislative initiative passed to the Commons for the time being. All this happened in a climate characterised by the Lords' declining efficiency, attendance and productivity – symptoms of a climate of sterility which mirrored both the Queen's own condition and some of her most cherished ambitions.

Part Three: Assessment

7   Conclusion

When the reigns of the first four Tudors are viewed together, and within the broader context of English parliamentary history, they (and not just the dramatic decade of the 1530s) constitute one of the more important phases in the development of Parliament. Whilst some of the changes, especially those between 1529 and 1540, may have been so novel and significant as to warrant the label 'revolutionary', they can also be regarded, to a certain extent at least, as the culmination of a long historical process. Furthermore, change was not a characteristic of the early Tudor parliaments alone. Henry VII's assemblies were the legatees of over 200 years of intermittent existence – intermittent because they were activated only when the monarch required them. Nevertheless, whilst parliaments had always been more often dormant than active, and indeed continued to be so, they had never been static nor in danger of stagnation or eclipse. Indeed, by 1485 they had travelled far from their emergence during the mid-thirteenth-century baronial opposition to Henry III, in their functions, composition, and authority. Certain fundamentals, however, had not altered. Parliaments continued to be royal occasions, brought into being and terminated by the King, designed to serve him, and during which he was the dominant force. And, just as both continuity and change had been features of the past history of parliaments, so they were to be characteristic of parliamentary history during the reigns of the first four Tudors. Undue concentration on the elements of novelty, especially during and after the 1530s, produces a history which lacks balance and perspective and is a distortion of the reality.

However, it is just as important not to belittle the extent and significance of change. Indeed, changes of far-reaching importance had already taken place between the inception of parliaments in the thirteenth century and Henry VII's accession. The House of Commons had been fully incorporated into Parliament, and it had moved from mere petitioner to co-equal partner of the House of Lords in the business of law-making. Secondly, despite continued contemporary references to 'the High Court of Parliament', its early curial character had progressively diminished, and it now provided legislative rather than judicial solutions to urgent causes, the grievances of the subject, and petty matters pertaining to individuals or localities. Moreover, whilst it is correct to describe parliaments as occasions, it is equally valid to refer to them as meetings of the Parliament – in other words an institution with its own bureaucracy, archives, fixed venue, and procedures which were in the gradual process of standardisation and refinement. Admittedly its sessions were usually short, and its meetings intermittent, sometimes even infrequent, as in 1497–1510 and 1515–29. Nevertheless its bureaucratic organisation and archives remained in permanent existence and provided an element of continuity. And whenever Parliament was re-activated it proceeded to exercise an authority in taxation and legislation which was both unequalled and unimpaired by even lengthy dormant periods. If Parliament was, more often than not, asleep, there was not the remotest possibility of it being laid to permanent rest, as the French *États Généraux* were after 1614–15 and the *Cortes* of Castile after 1665. It was far too important and valuable to the crown for that to occur. The record speaks for itself. During the sixteenth century, the Castilian *Cortes*, for example, was summoned on thirty-six occasions and the *États Généraux* on only six. The infrequency of the latter was a commentary on its very limited value to the French crown. And the *Cortes*, which had no legislative function beyond the right to petition, was invariably called just to obtain its assent to taxation. In contrast the twenty-three English parliaments, meeting in forty-four sessions between 1485 and 1558, were used to settle the affairs of crown and kingdom by stabilising Henry VII's position, resolving his son's 'great matter', enacting the Edwardian Reformation and then reversing it in the following reign. The vitality and usefulness of the institution were unquestionable, and its future was never in doubt.

During the pre-Reformation parliaments, there were innovations, as well as the continuation or conclusion of medieval developments. The King's cavalier practice of tampering with Commons' bills, after they had passed both Houses, came to an end. A parliamentary office, housing the original parchment Acts, was established. Printed statutes, and a systematically-compiled Lords' Journal with attendance register, were regularly produced. The necessity of the Commons' assent to a new law, together with the recognition that Parliament was not a Continental-style assembly of estates, received judicial confirmation. These changes amounted to no sudden and dramatic revolution. They were simply staging-posts on the long road of institutional growth, in which Kings, Councillors, members of both Houses, judges, and parliamentary bureaucrats all played a part. The same was true of the fundamental change in the relationship between the King, on the one hand, and the Lords and Commons on the other. For two centuries parliaments had been a 'coming-together' and parley between the King and his great ecclesiastical and temporal feudatories, who were increasingly afforced by representatives of the shires and boroughs. In other words, they were meetings of a King and his Parliament. However, change crept in, slowly and even imperceptibly. Before the Reformation Parliament (1529–36) set in train thirty years of turbulent politics and dramatic developments the relationship had altered. The crown had become a part of the institution, which, as a consequence, became a trinity of King, Lords, and Commons: King-in-Parliament instead of King *and* Parliament.

In short, there were changes, some of considerable significance, in the pre-Reformation parliaments. Yet they amounted not to a digression, but rather to a culmination of more than two centuries of development. This continuity was also characteristic of the parliaments of the 1530s, albeit to a lesser extent. Certainly they performed great deeds. They enacted into law a schism; they confirmed a God-given supremacy over the Church, vested in the King; they authorised the production of a vernacular Bible, and sanctioned a corpus of Catholic doctrine for the Church of England. They abolished monasteries and franchises, empowered Henry VIII to do the same with chantries, united England and Wales, and passed a considerable volume of law reform and commonweal legislation. As the statutory authority of Parliament probed into everyone's life, contemporaries must have been acutely aware of the dramatic and rapid pace of change. No less important than Parliament's impact on society was the impact of its activity upon the nature of the institution itself. The customary limits on statute, which had formerly prevented it from trespassing on the prohibited territory of matters spiritual and property rights, were thrown down as statute became omnicompetent. As a consequence, King-in-Parliament became sovereign. In other words, the King, together with his Lords and Commons, could achieve objectives which were beyond the scope of his prerogative when he acted alone. As Henry VIII informed both Houses in 1542, 'We at no time stand so highly in our estate royal as in the time of Parliament'. There were other, concurrent, changes. For example, the crown increased the Commons' membership and, as a consequence of the statutes which dissolved the monasteries, it created a permanent secular majority in the Lords. At the same time the relationship between the two Houses began to fluctuate according to political circumstances. The legislative initiative shifted from one House to the other, depending on the placement of the King's chief minister and on the degree of trust which the monarch placed in each chamber. Such variations, however, were ephemeral. Throughout the 1530s, and indeed for most of the century (apart from that brief lapse in 1553–5), the House of Lords remained the more orderly, organised, prestigious, influential, better-served, and efficient chamber. Continuity sat alongside change.

This was also true of those who actively participated in the parliamentary process, from the King downwards. Before, and during, the assemblies of 1529–58, they all continued to politick to achieve their particular ends. If, in the crucible of the Reformation, radical royal policies sometimes engendered heat, disagreement, and even conflict, that is hardly surprising in an institution with a wide competence before the 1530s and the capacity to do anything thereafter. As Parliament was the only place in which the great affairs of the kingdom could be resolved, and their resolution be embodied in the highest form of law, so it was there alone that opponents could prevent their implementation into law. Indeed, royal aspirations were sometimes frustrated: in 1545, for instance, the King's Secretary, Sir William Petre, wrote to William Paget that 'The bill of books . . . is finally dashed in the Commons House, as are divers others'. However, he added that 'I hear not that his Majesty is much miscontented' (**2**, vol. XX, pt 2, no. 1030). An experienced politician like Henry learned to take the rough with the smooth. But for most of the time the crown continued to get what it wanted, even if it took Henry VIII seven years to obtain his feudal rights by the Statute of Uses, Edwardian government had to overcome stiff resistance to its religious measures in the Lords, and Mary thought better of proposing to Parliament that her consort Philip should be crowned. More serious, so far as royal authority was concerned, was the way in which post-Henrician governments carelessly allowed the personal headship of the Church to be transformed into a parliamentary title. Unscrupulous Edwardian ruling circles also continued the process, begun by Henry VIII in the 1540s, of squandering the enormous financial assets acquired by the crown in the previous decade. These inroads into royal authority and financial solvency, however, were the consequences of short-sighted, inept, or corrupt government and not of parliamentary hostility or resistance.

Parliamentary developments were affected in other ways too by the consequences of the 1530s. Firstly, the composition of the institution changed, as the abbots disappeared from the Lords, bishops became victims of the shifts in Reformation politics, the nobility became increasingly *nouveau* and plutocratic, and Henry and his successors added new seats to the Commons. Secondly, there was a continued refinement of parliamentary procedures and a consolidation of the Commons' privileges and liberties. Above all, there was the increasing ease with which King-in-Parliament employed omnicompetent statute to effect alterations in religion, order the commonwealth, serve the crown, and consolidate the social supremacy of the landed governing class. And if some of Parliament's members were learning the arts of opposition, to be employed when the occasion required, royal government was, at the same time, perfecting its techniques of management.

It is true that a new, abrasive element – ideological conflict – penetrated England and Parliament, as the Continental Protestant Reformation made its way along the trade routes into London and the governing class. In addition, the political ambitions of Tudor politicians were worked out more overtly in parliaments under a boy-King and a Queen who was an inept manager. Despite these handicaps, the crown continued to engineer statutory changes in religion, and it also established the novel principle that it could justifiably request extraordinary revenue in ordinary peacetime circumstances. Although the sessions of 1553–5 in particular were troubled and troublesome, Mary's last Parliament was in the process of dutifully voting her a tax when she died. Throughout the early Tudor period, then, Parliament remained a royal institution, called to service the crown. Disagreements, conflicts, and criticisms notwithstanding, it was still an instrument of unity, not division. And it continued to be a communion of crown and governing elite, acting as partners in the management of the kingdom. Parliament also concerned itself with commonwealth matters and the rights and 'liberties' of the subject. In all of these ways it served the interests of both the monarchy and the wider community of the realm. If the Castilian *Cortes*, consisting of thirty-six townsmen elected by eighteen cities and towns, could call itself 'the kingdom', how much more appropriate it would have been for the English Parliament to describe itself in that way.

Part Four: Documents

The records of the early Tudor parliaments provide much leaner fare for the interested reader or student, than those for their more fortunate counterparts whose preference or course of study is Elizabeth's reign or the early Stuarts. This is the result of a combination of circumstances. There are the inevitable accidents of survival, destruction, and disappearance, of which the most mysterious and serious are the loss of the Lords' Journals and original Acts for some sessions. To some extent, at least, this can be accounted for by the casual and haphazard way in which the parliamentary archives were managed. In November 1548, for example, Protector Somerset wrote to Sir Edward North, who had surrendered the Clerkship of the Parliaments eight years before, instructing him 'to deliver to Sir John Mason knight all such Acts of Parliament and other writings touching the same as, since the time you were Clerk of the Parliament, have out of their place remained in your custody' (**3**, vol. XI, 3852(b)). There has also been the occasional disaster, such as the parliamentary fire of 1834, which destroyed most of Westminster Palace and so many of the paper bills. And in addition there is the unavoidable archival consequence of the fact that we are studying Parliament at a crucial formative stage in its institutional development: this is reflected in the change in the content of the Parliament Roll in 1484, and the preservation of the original parchment Acts of Parliament at Westminster only from 1497.

Apart from the diary of the Colchester burgesses for the Parliament of 1485 (**26**), there is also a conspicuous lack of the private journals which so often add flesh to the bare bones of the official record of Elizabethan and early Stuart assemblies. Fortunately chroniclers including Edward VI himself (**17**), Edward Halle, who was also a parliamentary burgess in the Reformation Parliament and three later Henrician assemblies (**12**), and Ingulph (**28**) help to compensate for this deficiency. So does William Roper's biography of his father-in-law, Sir Thomas More (**31**). The compilations of antiquaries, such as William Lambarde (**33**) and Henry Scobell (**30**) and the law commentaries of Edward Coke (**6**), St German (**29**) and Spilman (**116**) shed light on parliamentary procedures and proceedings. Sometimes the parliamentary story is filled out by the correspondence of Thomas Cromwell (**20**), Bishop Gardiner (**21**), Simon Renard, the imperial ambassador at Mary I's Court (**1**), and other prominent men (**2, 14, 27, 82**). Together, these extracts open windows onto early Tudor parliaments: why they were called; how they went about their business; the growth of the institution's authority; the way in which men, from the King downwards, politicked to achieve their particular ends; and how royal, commonweal, and private interests were accommodated, especially in a period of rapid, dramatic, even revolutionary change. Finally, if the relative paucity of extant materials prevents the painting of a fully-rounded portrait, at least they provide a sketch both of an assembly which was a microcosm of the political nation and of the broad spectrum of human behaviour which its meetings exhibited.

document 1

The limited authority of statute

(a) *Christopher St German on the limited competence of statute, 1530*
[E]very man's law must be consonant to the law of God. And therefore the laws of princes, nor the commandments of prelates, the statutes of communities, nor yet the ordinance of the Church is not right wise nor obligatory but it be consonant to the law of God . . .

Christopher St German (**29**).

(b) *The De Facto Act, 1495, incorporates the (mistaken) notion that a statute can bind subsequent statutes.*
It be therefore ordained, enacted, and established by the King our sovereign lord, by advice and assent of the lords spiritual and temporal and commons in this present parliament assembled and by authority of the same, that from henceforth no manner of person nor persons . . . that attend upon the King . . . for the time being in his person and do him true and faithful service . . . in his wars within this land or without, that for the same . . true service of allegiance he or they be in no wise convict[ed] or attaint[ed] of high treason nor of other offences for that cause by act of parliament or otherwise by any process of law . . . And if any act or acts or other process of the law hereafter . . . be made contrary to this ordinance, that then

that act or acts or other processes of the law . . . stand and be utterly void.

11 Henry VII, Cap. 1 (**19**), vol. II, p. 568.

document 2

The omnicompetence of statute

(a) *1534. Sir Thomas More, at his trial, denies that statute can override the laws of God and the Church.*
'Forasmuch as, my lord', quoth he, 'this indictment is grounded upon an act of Parliament directly repugnant to the laws of God and His Holy Church, the supreme government of which, or of any part whereof, may no temporal prince presume by any law to take upon him, as rightfully belonging to the See of Rome, a spiritual pre-eminence by the mouth of Our Saviour himself, personally present upon the earth, only to Saint Peter and his successors, bishops of the same See, by special prerogative granted. It is therefore in law, amongst Christian men, insufficient to charge any Christian man.'

William Roper, *Life of Sir Thomas More* (**31**), p. 248.

(b) *1534. Statute and matters spiritual: the Act of Supremacy*
Albeit the king's majesty justly and rightly is and oweth to be the supreme head of the Church of England and so is recognised by the clergy of this realm in their convocations; yet never the less for corroboration and confirmation thereof, . . . be it enacted by authority of this present parliament that the king . . . his heirs and successors . . . shall be taken, accepted, and reputed the only supreme head in earth of the Church of England . . .

26 Henry VIII (1534), Cap. 1. (**19**), vol. III, p. 492.

(c) *1536. Statute and property rights: the dissolution of the lesser monasteries*
For as much as manifest sin, vicious, carnal and abominable living is daily used and committed amongst the little and small abbeys, priories, and other religious houses of monks, canons and nuns, where the congregation of such religious persons is under the number of xii persons . . . the said lords and commons . . . most humbly desire the king's highness that it may be enacted by authority of this present parliament, that his majesty shall have and enjoy to him

and to his heirs forever all and singular such monasteries . . . which have not in lands . . . above the clear yearly value of two hundred pounds . . .

27 Henry VIII (1536), Cap. 28 (**19**), vol. III, p. 575.

document 3
How parliaments enacted statute: the three-reading procedure

(a) *1485. The Commons in the pre-Reformation parliaments*
The xth day of November there was read a bill for the subsidy between the king and the merchants, which bill was examined amongst us and other divers persons and no conclusion.

The Colchester parliamentary diary of 1485 (**26**), p. 186.

(b) *1515. Friday, 9 March. The Lords in the pre-Reformation parliaments*
Item today the bill concerning widows is read the first time . . .
Item the bill concerning the watermen is read the second time . . .
Item the bill concerning exchange is committed to Master Pigot, Master Palmes and Master Carell for revision.

(**18**), vol. I, p. 30.

(c) *1554–55. Passage of the Bill to Reform Excess in Apparel, 1 & 2 Philip and Mary*
House of Lords
12 January: Today is read the 1st and 2nd times the bill for the reformation of excess in apparel, and committed to Master Dyer, serjeant at law, to engross it [i.e. write the paper bill onto parchment].
14 January: Today is read the bill for the reformation of excess in apparel, and the whole house assented, and sent to the commons by Sir Richard Reed and Master Armstead.
House of Commons
14 January: L1, 2. The bill to avoid excess of apparel – Mr. Pollard [Pollard is named as the chairman of the committee to scrutinise and, if necessary, to revise the bill.]
L3. The bill to avoid excess of apparel, with three new provisos – *jud'm*. ['L' indicates that the bill had come from the Lords. '*Jud'm*'

is the abbreviated form of '*judicium*' = judgement. It recorded the Commons' assent.]

House of Lords

16 January: Touching the reformation of excess in apparel with three new provisos added by the commons, and 1st, 2nd and 3rd readings, *conclusa est* [and is passed] with the dissenting voices of Lords Burgh and Darcy of Chiche.

Lords' Journals (**18**), vol. I, pp. 488, 490; *Commons' Journals* (**32**), vol. I, p. 41.

document 4

Parliamentary privilege

1523. Speaker More's petition to the King for freedom of speech

Mine other humble request, most excellent prince, is this. Forasmuch as there be of your commons . . . a great number which are after the accustomed manner appointed in the common house to treat and advise of the common affairs among themselves apart, and . . . there hath been as due diligence in sending up . . . the most discreet persons . . . that men could esteem meet thereunto . . . yet . . . it often happeneth that, likewise, as much folly is uttered with painted, polished speech, so many boisterous and rude in language see deep indeed and give right substantial counsel . . . It may therefore like your most abundant grace . . . to give all your commons here assembled your most gracious licence and pardon, freely, without doubt of your dreadful displeasure, every man to discharge his conscience, and boldly in every thing incident among us to declare his advice.

William Roper, *Life of Sir Thomas More* (**31**), pp. 203–5.

document 5

The Lords' membership

(a) *1514. A victorious soldier receives his reward*

The king . . . commanded that Sir Edward Stanley, second son of Thomas earl of Derby, should be proclaimed lord for such valiant acts as he did against the Scots at the battle of Branxton [Flodden], where James king of Scots was slain, and because he won the hill or mount against the Scots, and overcame all them which came against him . . . and also in consideration that his ancestors bare in their crest the eagle, named him the lord Mounteagle . . .

(**50**), vol. IX, Appendix F, p. 44.

(b) *1536. Nobility is identified with 'Peerage of Parliament'*
[*Lord Chancellor Audley to Viscount Lisle, Lord Deputy of Calais, 14 May 1536*]
The king's highness hath summoned his parliament to be holden at Westminster the Thursday in Whitsun week next coming. Wherefore I send your lordship one writ for your summons to be there. Nevertheless you shall not need to come, unless you have further knowledge of the king's pleasure that his grace is content that you shall be absent from your charge at Calais. But I send you the writ, because it is the order that every nobleman should have his writ of summons of a parliament.

(**22**), p. 166.

(c) *1553. The heirs of nobles are summoned by Royal Grace*
[*The Duke of Northumberland to Sir William Cecil, 19 January 1553*]
It is only upon the grace and favour of his majesty [that heirs apparent can be called] by writ, to sit and have voice in his highness' high court of parliament . . . for no man's son from the highest to the lowest degree being not of the blood royal can claim any place to sit there . . . And for the heirs apparent, if it shall please his highness to call any [they shall] be the better able to occupy the places [of their] parents.

(**27**), 10/18, fol. 8.

(d) *1559. The exclusion of minors*
No peer is called to sit as a member of that great council, or to have his free voice, until he have accomplished his full age, unless by the special grace of the prince, and that very rarely, unless they be near upon the age of twenty at the least.

(**9**), p. 11.

(e) *1547 and 1553. The exclusion of royal prisoners*
[*Bishop Stephen Gardiner protests from prison, c. November 1547*]
I am bold to write these [letters], wherewith to put your Grace

[Protector Somerset] in remembrance of mine estate in prison . . . without knowledge of any just cause wherefore, and with knowledge, by course of time, that now the parliament is begun, whereof I am a member, unless my fault had cut me off. And whereunto I was called by writ, which I received before my coming hither, where I would also gladly do my duty, as I am bounden, if I were not detained and bounden in prison from my liberty . . .

(**21**), p. 410.

(f) *1553. Bishop Taylor of Lincoln is removed to the Tower of London*
Item the Vth day of the same month began the parliament; and when they were in the parliament house the bishop of Lincoln . . . his parliament robe was taken from him and he was committed to the Tower.

(**23**), pp. 84–5.

document 6

The burden of parliaments

1534.5 April. John, Lord Latimer, to Thomas Cromwell
As I have been at every prorogation of parliament nearly these four years, which has been painful and chargeable to me, as I have not yet paid the king all that is due for the livery* of my lands, nor all the sums I am bound to pay by the wills of my father and my mother-in-law, I beg you will get me leave to tarry at home and be absent from the next prorogation. I shall be in better readiness to do the king service against the Scots when we in these parts are called upon. I send you a gelding by this bearer . . .

(**2**), vol. VI, no. 438.

document 7

The Commons' membership

(a) *1536. The enfranchisement of Calais*
From henceforth there shall be two able persons, dwelling and inhabiting within the said town of Calais, present at . . every parliament . . hereafter to be holden . . . to be elected and chosen in manner and form following, that is to say: two several writs to be made and the one of them to be directed unto the deputy and council

of . . . Calais, commanding them . . . to nominate, elect, and choose an able and discreet person inhabiting within the said town of Calais . . .; and one other writ to be directed unto the mayor, burgesses, and freemen of the commonalty of . . . Calais commanding them by authority of the same . . . to nominate, elect, and choose one other able and apt person inhabiting within the same town to be one other of the burgesses of . . . Calais.

27 Henry VIII, Cap. 63 (**19**), vol. III, p. 649.

(b) *1550 and 1553. The qualifications of members are questioned*
[*Francis Russell's father was promoted to the Earldom of Bedford on 19 January 1550. This resulted in a discussion about the right of an heir-apparent to a senior peerage to sit in the Commons.*]
21 January 1553. It is ordered that Sir Francis Russell, son and heir apparent of the now earl of Bedford, shall abide in this house in the state he was before.
13 Ocotber 1553. It is declared . . . that Alexander Nowell, being prebendary* in Westminster, and thereby having voice in the convocation-house,* cannot be a member of this house; and so agreed by the house; and the queen's writ to be directed for another burgess in that place.

(**32**), pp. 15, 27.

document 8
Two carpet-baggers: 1510 and 1555

(a) *1510. 13 January. Grimsby (Lincolnshire) accedes to the request of a local magnate*
It shall be lawful to Sir William Tyrwhitt, knight [to admit] Sir Robert Wingfield, knight, for to be burgess of the parliament for the town with himself or else to admit . . . the said Sir Robert Wingfield . . . with John Heneage.

(**47**), vol. III, p. 504.

(b) *1555. 28 September. Liverpool [Lancashire] elects two outsiders*
Wherein [Sir Richard Sherborn] knight and steward to the noble Earl, Lord Edward, Earl of Derby, was elected to be the one burgess for Liverpool and [blank] a place left open for the other to be nominated by Master [blank] Rochester . . . [*Sir Robert Rochester*

*was the Chancellor of the Duchy of Lancaster, within which Liverpool lay.
His choice was John Beaumont, who had been a prominent Edwardian civil
servant.*]

(**47**), vol. I, p. 124

Aristocratic patrons

document 9

(a) *1550. 20 January. An obliging patron: The Earl of Bedford writes to
'my very loving friends Mr. John Tukfield, Mayor of Exeter, and his brethren'*
[Informs them that he is going away on the King's business and
that he has requested his] loving friends the two burgesses for Exeter, who have behaved themselves very thankfully in the service of
you all, not to remain at Westminster during my absence, but to
repair thither on my return, and this for the more sure furthering of
all the city's suits, which all my lords of the Council favour the
more, for that your faithful constancy and defending of the late
rebels [during the 'prayer book rebellion' of 1549] in those parts
from your city.

(**14**), 73, p. 22.

(b) *1548/9. A disruptive patron: Thomas Seymour's sinister politicking.
Edward VI's testimony, 1549.*
The lord admiral came to me at the last parliament and desired me to
write a thing for him. I asked him what. He said it was non ill. It is
for the queen's matters. [Seymour had married Henry VIII's widow
Queen Catherine Parr.] I said if it were good the lords would allow
it; if it were ill I will not write in it. Then he said they would take
[it] in better part if I wrote.

Bodleian Library, Rawlinson *MS. D.* 1070.

1549. 17 January.
[Seymour] induced the king's majesty without the advice or
knowledge either of the lord protector or council to write letters of
his devising to the parliament, minding by colour of the same to
have set sedition in the realm, and thereupon . . . intended to have
made the blackest parliament that ever was in England.

1549. 23 February. Charges against Seymour.
You had determined to have come into the common house yourself,
and there with your fautours [supporters or clients] and adherents
before prepared to have made a broil or tumult and uproar.

1549. 24 February.
[Seymour admitted] that he had thought to have made suit to the
parliament house [to be named governor of the King's person] and
he had the names of all the lords, and totted them whom he thought
he might have to his purpose to labour them.

(**8**), vol. II, pp. 237, 248, 259.

1549. The Marquess of Dorset's examination.
[Seymour declared that] 'If I be thus used, they speak of a black
parliament, by God's precious soul, I will make the blackest parliament that ever was in England'. To whom my Lord Clinton
answered, 'If you speak such words, you shall lose my lord [Lord
Protector Somerset, Seymour's brother] utterly, and undo yourself'.

[Seymour said] 'I hear say that there shall be a subsidy granted to
the king this parliament'. 'What subsidy?' said I. 'Marry', sayeth
he, 'every man that hath sheep shall pay to his Grace twopence
yearly for every sheep, and to that I will never grant unto it'.
'Why?', said I. 'You were better grant such a subsidy than one out
of your lands, and less charge it should be to you, for well I wot, it
shall be lesse charge to me'. 'Well', said he, 'do as you will, I will
not'.

(**13**), vol. I, pp. 75–6; (**15**), pt I, no. 300.

document 10
The Privy Council attempts to influence an election

1553. January. Edward VI's letter to the Sheriffs
Trusty and well-beloved, we greet you well. Forasmuch as we have,
for divers good considerations, caused a summonition for a parliament to be made . . . we have thought it meet . . . that in the election of such persons as shall be sent to the parliament . . . there be
good regard had, that the choice be made of men of gravity and
knowledge in their own countries and towns, fit for their under-

standing and qualities, to be in such a great council . . . And yet, nevertheless, our pleasure is, that where our privy council, or any of them, within their jurisdictions, in our behalf, shall recommend men of learning and wisdom, in such case their directions be regarded and followed . . .

(**81**), vol. II, pt II, pp. 64–5.

document 11
Attendance and absenteeism: the House of Commons

(a) *1515. The licensing of absentees*
For so much as commonly . . . . divers knights of shire, citizens for cities, burgesses for boroughs, and barons of the Cinque ports [a purely honorary title bestowed on members elected for Dover, Rye, New Romney, Hythe, Hastings, Sandwich and Winchelsea] long time before the end of . . . parliament of their own authority depart and goeth home, whereby . . . great and weighty matters are many times greatly delayed, . . . be it enacted by the king . . . the lords spiritual and temporal and the commons in this present parliament assembled that, from henceforth none . . . of them . . . do not depart from the same parliament . . . till the same parliament be fully finished . . . except he or they so departing have licence of the speaker and commons . . . upon pain to every of them so departing . . . to lose . . . their wages.

6 Henry VIII, Cap. 16 (**19**), vol. III, p. 134.

(b) *1554/5. Actions against absentees: calling the roll.*
Friday, 27 April 1554: It is ordered that the house shall be called on Monday afternoon.
Friday, 11 January 1555: The house was this day called; and ordered to be called again on Monday next.

It is a common policy to say upon the Wednesday that the house shall be called on Saturday, and upon Saturday to say it shall be called on Wednesday; and so from day to day by fear thereof to keep the company together.

Informations preferred by the attorney-general against thirty-nine of the house of commons for departing without licence, contrary to the king's inhibition in the beginning of the parliament; whereof six being timorous burgesses . . . submitted themselves to their fines.

(**32**), pp. 35, 41; (**33**), p. 66; (**6**), pt. 4, p. 17.

document 12
Attendance and absenteeism: the House of Lords

(a) *1547. 5 October. A royal servant seeks advice*
It may please your lordships also to be advertised that I have received a writ for mine attendance at the parliament, where I am desirous to be. And having a weighty charge on these west marches with his majesty's subjects, and now a number of Scotsmen and a great country won to his highness' said service, I beseech your lordships that I may receive your honourable commandments by this post what I shall do in this behalf. And Almighty God have your lordships ever more in his most blessed preservation.

Thomas Lord Wharton, Warden of the West Marches, to the Privy Council, (**27**), 15/1, fol. 31.

(b) *1541. 21 December. Instructions from the Privy Council*
As by letters of Westmorland and otherwise, it was signified that the king of Scots was come to the Borders, letters were sent to [the Earls of] Westmorland and Cumberland to remain at home, for the safety of the Borders, and not repair to parliament.

(**2**), vol. XVI, pt I, no. 1464.

(c) *1534. A bishop is ordered home*
I was at that time in the household of Cuthbert Tunstal, bishop of Durham, who . . . was considered likely to stand out against the king's unjust desires [i.e. his divorce]. Wherefore when we were on our road, and not far from London . . . Cromwell, who then managed everything under the king, sent the bishop a letter. In this . . . it was stated that, since on account of the inclemency of the winter weather and the difficulty of travelling a journey to a man of the bishop's age would be most insupportable, it had pleased his majesty . . . to grant him leave to stay at home. While the bishop was in great doubt what to do in this dilemma . . . behold the next day there arrived another letter, not now from Cromwell, but from the king himself, which not merely permitted but ordered him to return to his diocese.

The recollections of Richard Hilliard, (**82**), p. 191.

document 13

Supply

(a) 1504. Henry VII requests a Feudal Aid and is refused – an apocryphal story
[Thomas More] was in the latter time of King Henry VII made a burgess of the parliament, wherein there were by the king demanded (as I have heard reported) about three fifteenths* for the marriage of his eldest daughter . . . At the last debating whereof he made such arguments and reasons there against, that the king's demands thereby were clean overthrown. So that one of the king's privy chamber, named Master Tyler, being present thereat, brought word to the king out of the parliament house that a beardless boy had disappointed all his purpose. Whereupon the king, conceiving great indignation towards him, could not be satisfied until he had some way revenged it . . . [His] grace devised a causeless quarrel against his father, keeping him in the Tower until he had made him pay to him an hundred pounds fine.

William Roper, Life of Sir Thomas More (**31**), p. 199.

document 14

1553–4. Powerful men plead their causes at the Commons' Bar

1553. 4 December. The Duke of Norfolk
The duke of Norfolk came into the house, and made request that the house would pass his bill, showing that, for the causes betwixt him and the patentees, he would abide the order of certain lords and other, to whom the matter was compromitted; and if the arbiters did not agree, then the queen to make a final end as it should please her highness.

1554. 18 April. Bishop Tunstal of Durham
The Bishop of Durham came present into the house, and declared his whole cause, forcing his bill, and his trouble by the duke of Northumberland, and required the house to consider the bill.

1554. 19 April. Arguments upon the bill for the Bishop of Durham
Upon the question for the bill, the house did divide; and the number that said yea to the bill were two hundred and one persons; and

against the bill but one hundred and twenty; and so the bill passed with yea – *Judicium*.

(**32**), vol. I, pp. 32, 34.

document 15
1523. The productivity of parliaments – a cynical observation

August 17: Thomas Cromwell to John Creke
I amongst other have endured a parliament which continued by the space of seventeen whole weeks, where we communed of war, peace, strife, contention, debate, murmur, grudge, riches, poverty, penury, truth, falsehood, justice, equity, deceit, oppression, magnanimity, activity, force, attemprance, treason, murder, felony . . . and also how a commonwealth might be edified and also continued within our realm. Howbeit in conclusion we have done as our predecessors have been wont to do, that is to say, as well as we might, and left where we began.

(**20**), vol. I, p. 313.

document 16
The Lords' formidable presence: a Joint Conference

Such as were sent from [the House of Commons] being come hither . . . at the time and place appointed by the lords . . . the lords came to them all at once, and not scatteringly, which might take from their gravity, and prevent their places. The lords did sit there covered, the commons did stand bare, during the time of the conference.

(**30**), pp. 30–1.

document 17
The Lords apply pressure on the Commons in matters of lay taxation

(a) 1515. 10 February.
Today the lord chancellor, the archbishop of York, the bishop of Winchester, the bishop of Durham, the duke of Norfolk (lord treasurer), the earl of Surrey, the earl of Worcester, with other lords,

went down to the commons house, where the lord chancellor declared the cause of parliament's assembly and especially how the sums of money granted to his sacred majesty the king in the previous parliament [were] not yet paid . . .

(**18**), vol. I, p. 21.

(b) 1558. January.

Imprimis, the 24th day of [January] being the first day of the full parliament, it was moved from the lords spiritual and temporal unto the commons of this parliament, that 9 of the said lords, whereof 3 to be of the estate of earls, 3 of the state of the clergy, and 3 barons, should with the number of 21 of the most grave men of the said commons consult and deliberate upon some ways how the state of this realm might be preserved and defended from the malice and invasion of the enemy. According to which motion, 3 of every of the said estates and 21 of the said commons were specially appointed to travail in the device of this matter. And to the intent that no way or policy should be undevised or not thought upon, most commodious for this purpose, [the chosen] lords and commons separated and divided themselves in 3 parts or councils . . . And after the 3 several councils had consulted and devised upon this matter 3 days, the fourth day they all assembled together, and amongst themselves declared their several opinions and desires. And in conclusion all resolved that the only way to minister relief unto their majesties was to offer unto the same a certain mass of money . . .

(**27**), 11/12/31, fol. 67–67v.

(c) 1558. 14 November.

The lord chancellor, the lord treasurer, the duke of Norfolk, the earl of Shrewsbury, the earl of Pembroke, the bishops of Winchester, London, Lincoln, and Carlisle, the Viscount Montagu, the lord admiral, and the Lord William Howard, came into this house, sitting where the queen's privy council of this house use to sit. And the lord chancellor by his oration declared that, by necessity, for the safeguard of this realm from the French and Scots, a subsidy must be had, Mr. Speaker and the privy council then sitting from them on the lowest benches. And, after the declaration made, the lords departed.

(**32**), vol. I, p. 52.

document 18

The services of the legal assistants

(a) Drafting bills in preparation for a parliament
1551. 15 December. There were certain devices for laws delivered to
my learned council to pen, as by a schedule appeareth.

(**17**), p. 100.

(b) Drafting bills during a parliamentary session
1554. 24 December. Yesterday, the same lords and judges returned
and with much difficulty it was at length settled that all the laws
made at the time of the schism against the papal authority should
be abrogated thus: that in the act of parliament, all those [laws]
which they have been able to collect are to be specified and to
remove all difficulty, they have placed at the end of a general repeal
. . . [an acknowledgement] that the Church property is to remain
in the hands of its present English possessors.

(**4**), vol. V, no. 975, p. 598.

(c) Lending advice
[Robert Aske] remembers that Lord Darcy said that, in any matter
touching the king's prerogative, the custom of the lords' house was
that they should have, upon their request, a copy of the bill to be
scanned by their learned counsel in case they could perceive anything prejudicial to the prerogative or, if it were between party and
party, if the bill were not prejudicial to the commonwealth.

Aske's examination, 11 April 1537 (**2**), vol. XII, pt. I, no. 901,
p. 410.

(d) Scrutinising and revising bills
1547. 9 November. Today *prime vice lecta est billa* [a first reading was
given to the bill], for continuance of processes after the death of any
king, and committed to Master Hinde [serjeant at law] and Justice
Hales.

1547. 19 November. Item, the aforesaid day, *prima vice lecta est billa*,
for the exercising of the ecclesiastical jurisdictions, and committed
to [Sir Edward] Montague, Justice, Lord Chief Baron [the Chief

Justice of the Court of the Exchequer], Master Hales, serjeant at law, Mr. Attorney and Solicitor.

1554. 31 December. Item *secunda vice lecta est billa* [a second reading was given to the bill], that the counterfeiting of strange coins, being current within this realm, or the bringing in of the same, shall be treason, and committed to the chief justice of common pleas and Master Dyer, serjeant at law.

(**18**), vol. I, pp. 295, 299, 482.

document 19

Preparation of a legislative programme

(a) 1535. 'Remembrances' of a royal servant (author unknown, but probably Thomas Cromwell)
Item. Some way to be devised betwixt this and next session by which young men should be restrained from marriage till they be of potent age, and tall and puissant persons stayed from marriage of old widows. Some good way to be devised for restraint and utter extinction of the abuses of lawyers. Some reasonable way to be devised for the king's wards and primer seisin [This refers to the impending bill of uses. See also pp. 69–70, and **doc. 28**.] That it may please the king that an act may pass that strangers shall pay no more custom for merchandise (except wool) than Englishmen, which will be a great wealth to the realm and a singular profit to the king. That an act may be made against usury, which is cloaked by pretence of law. That an act may be made that merchants shall employ their goods continually in traffic and not in purchasing lands . . .

(**2**), vol. IX, no. 725 (ii).

(b) 1554. 23 February. A meeting of Queen Mary's Privy Council
The names of all such as be appointed for the purposes following: To consider what laws shall be established in this parliament and to name men that shall make the books thereof: my lord chancellor, my lord treasurer, my lord of Durham, my lord Paget, Mr. Petre, Mr. Baker, Mr. Hare.

(**8**), vol. IV, pp. 197–9.

document 20
Conciliar management of Commons' elections (see also doc. 10)

1554. Queen Mary I's letter to the sheriffs
These [letters] shall be to will and command you that, for withstanding such malice as the devil worketh by his ministers, for the maintenance of heresies and seditions, ye now, on our behalf, admonish such our good loving subjects, as by order of our writs should, within that county, choose knights, citizens, and burgesses, to repair from thence to this our parliament, to be of their inhabitants, as the old laws require, and of the wise, grave, and catholic sort, such as indeed mean the true honour of God, with the prosperity of the commonwealth.

(**81**), vol. III, pt I, p. 245.

document 21
Henry VIII as a manager (see also doc. 27)

(a) 1531. Henry lends 'a helping hand'
1 March. The Imperial Ambassador, Chapuys, to Emperor Charles V
The king had not yet been at the parliament since it recommenced, till late yesterday, when he remained an hour and a half or two hours in the house of lords, and did not go down to that of the commons. He expressed to them his desire for justice and the defence of the kingdom; and afterwards desired them to take into consideration certain liberties [privileges] of the Church in this kingdom by which malefactors had hitherto [enjoyed] full immunity . . .

(**2**), vol. V, no. 120.

(b) 1532. Henry meets a Commons' Delegation
2 May. Chapuys to Charles V
The king is again soliciting the estates for an aid for the fortification of the Scotch frontier. Two worthy men dared to say openly that the fortification was needless . . . and that the best fortification was to maintain justice in the kingdom and friendship with the emperor; and to this end the estates should petition the king to take back his wife, and treat her well; otherwise the kingdom would be ruined, as the emperor could do them more harm than any other, and would not abandon the rights of his aunt [Catherine of Aragon] . . . These

words were well taken by all present, except two or three, and nothing was concluded about the aid. The king was displeased, sent for the majority of the deputies and made them a long speech in justification of his conduct in the divorce. He told them it was not a matter in which they ought to interfere, and in a most gracious manner promised to support them against the Church . . . The estates have now granted a fifteenth which . . . only amounts to £28,000.

(2), vol. V, no. 989.

(c) 1545. 24 December. Henry VIII addresses the two houses of parliament. Sir William Petre to Sir William Paget

This morning, being Christmas Even, 24 December, parliament was prorogued until 4 November next, by the king in person. After hearing the proposition of the [Commons'] speaker, a great piece of which consisted in laud of his highness, the king required my lord chancellor, whose office has ever been to make answer for the king, to permit him to answer himself; and did so with a gravity so sententiously, so kingly, or rather fatherly, as peradventure to you that hath been used to his daily talks should have been no great wonder (and yet saw I some that hear him often enough largely water their plants), but to us, that have not heard him often, was such a joy and marvellous comfort as I reckon this day one of the happiest of my life.

(2), vol. XX, pt 2, no. 1030.

document 22
1547. Privy Councillors labour to avoid conflict

Whereas in the last parliament, among other articles contained in the act for colleges and chantry lands to be given unto his highness, it was also inserted that the lands pertaining to all guilds and brotherhoods within this realm should pass unto his Majesty by way of like gift, at which time divers then being of the lower house did not only reason and argue against that article for the guildable lands, but also incensed many others to hold with them, amongst the which none were stiffer nor more busily went about to impugn the said article than the burgesses for Lynn and Coventry . . . In respect of which their allegations and great labour made herein unto the House, such of his highness's council as were of the same house there present thought it very likely and apparent that not only that article for the guildable lands should be dashed, but also that the whole body of the act might either sustain peril or hindrance . . . unless by some good policy the principal speakers against the passing of that article might be stayed. Whereupon they, pondering . . . how the guildable lands throughout this realm amounted to no small yearly value, which by the article aforesaid were to be accrued to his majesty's possessions of the crown, thought it better to stay and content them of Lynn and Coventry by granting to them to have and enjoy their guild lands, . . . as they did before, than through their means, on whose importune labour and suggestion the great part of the lower house rested, to have the article defaced, and so his Majesty to forgo the whole guild lands throughout the realm. And for these respects, and also for avoiding of the proviso which the said burgesses would have had added for the guilds to this article, which might have ministered occasion to others to have laboured for the like, they resolved that certain of his highness' councillors being of the lower house, should persuade with the said burgesses of Lynn and Coventry to desist from further speaking or labouring against the said article, upon promise to them that, if they meddled no further against it, his Majesty, once having the guildable lands granted unto him by the act as it was penned unto him, should make them over a new grant of the lands pertaining then unto their guilds, etc., to be had and used to them as afore. Which thing the said councillors did execute as was devised, and thereby stayed the speakers against it, so as the act passed with the clause for guildable lands accordingly . . . .

(**8**), vol. II, pp. 193–5.

document 23
The golden bonds of Habsburg patronage

(a) 1554. 24 February. Imperial Ambassador Simon Renard to Emperor Charles V

We talked with [the Queen] about the favours she might bestow on certain of her most faithful subjects who had influence to win over others, and said that your Majesty had instructed us to show some liberality where it might seem advisable . . . in order to make friends for his Highness [Prince Philip, who became Queen Mary's husband on 25 July 1554], and also to consider to whom some pension might be given . . .

Paget conferred with the queen on the above point and sent us

... the names of the men who might have pensions, or receive chains (of gold). We did not definitely take Paget's advice, but thought it well to conciliate the others by talking over the matter with the chancellor [Gardiner] and the comptroller [Sir Robert Rochester], who have also given us a list of names in writing, with the sums appended, in accordance with which I ... have had 4,000 crowns melted down for chains, and the other 1,000 shall be distributed in money in the most effective manner possible ...

As for the above mentioned pensions, it is true that the sums specified in the note are large, but ... the names are those of leading men [and] ... influential members of the council ... If pensions are to be offered to them, they may easily be suppressed later on, and the money may be raised by extraordinary taxation over here.

(b) 1554. 13 March. Renard to Prince Philip

Parliament has been convoked for next April to settle all these matters and pass the articles of the marriage treaty; and if the nobles are conciliated by·pensions and liberalities there will be no need to fear the people.

(c) 1554. 3 April. Renard to the Emperor

As for parliament, it was opened yesterday ... Certainly, Sire, if the pensions had already been distributed before his Highness's coming [to England] it would have been a means of making the English do as one liked, for they are a nation that has to be kept friendly by means of gifts and liberalities ...

(d) 1554. June (?). Notes for Prince Philip's guidance in England

Item, in order favourably to dispose the principal members of parliament and render his Highness's coming secure, the ambassador has offered pensions of 2,000 English crowns ... to the earls of Pembroke, Arundel, Derby, and Shrewsbury; of 1,000 crowns to my Lords Dacre, the high treasurer, the comptroller, Secretary Petre, and the lord warden; and of 500 crowns to Southwell, Waldegrave, Englefield, the deputies of Calais and Guisnes. [All of these pensioners were Privy Councillors and/or prominent royal servants.]

(1), vol. XII, pp. 140–1, 143, 150, 201–2, 295.

document 24
Parliamentary politicking (see also doc. 9(b))

(a) 1553. London's preparations
Item, it was agreed that the several bills devised and read here this day by Mr. Recorder to be enacted by parliament, for and concerning the assize of firewood and the conveyance thereof to the City, and the putting down of iron mills within a certain compass of the City shall with all diligence be put forward as they were here reformed.

(**7**), 12, fol. 454v.

(b) 1553. Exeter's preparations
Remembrances for the parliament (probably drafted by Richard Prestwood, one of Exeter's parliamentary burgesses)
To make suit for the gift of the plate as well for that is given already to the haven by the parishioners, as also for the residue of the whole plate of the parishes of St Peter with all the bells within the county of the city of Exeter. [The city was trying to raise funds for the cutting of a new watercourse to the sea – in particular from the goods which had been confiscated from churches in the cause of 'pure and simple religion'.] . . . Item, to deliver to my lord privy seal [Exeter's patron, the Earl of Bedford] a tun of Gascon wine. . . . Item, that if any bill be put in the parliament for bells, plate, or ornaments of the churches, then to cause friends to be made to have all the plate, bells, and ornaments within the county of Exeter towards the reparation and making the new haven or at least to have a proviso for that [which] is given by the parishes to the haven.

(**14**), 73, pp. 32–3.

(c) A feud has parliamentary repercussions
1549. 5 January. [first reading] The bill for sheriffs of England to be but one year. [The Earls of Cumberland were hereditary sheriffs of Westmorland.]

7 January. Thomas Jolye to the Earl of Cumberland.
[The bill] could not be otherwise than by the procurement of the Lord Wharton . . . albeit I doubt not but the same shall not proceed.

9 January. The bill for sheriffs of England to be but one year. [The bill proceeded no further.]

September
[The Earl of Cumberland's servants, Christopher Crackenthorpe and Thomas Allenfield, were riding to Mallerstang Forest] there to hunt and kill red deer for your said subject [the Earl, when Henry Wharton] son of the said Lord Wharton . . . with many others to the number of three hundred persons of the household, servants and adherents of the said Lord Wharton, riotously and unlawfully assembled and gathered together by procurement and commandment of the said Lord Wharton with force and armour . . . [and] forestalled your said orator's servants of their passage in the said highway and then and there sore menaced and threatened to beat [them] . . . and the said Sir Henry Wharton and the riotous persons aforesaid pursued after them . . . [Lord Wharton then kept his men] assembled together at Wharton all that day looking for the return of your said subject's servants from the said chase or forest . . . . They were in such dread . . . that they durst not return home, but for the . . . safeguard of their own lives they remained at Mallerstang that night. [This was only one of a whole series of incidents in the incessant feuding between Cumberland and Lord Wharton.]

1558. 3 February.
Item, is read a bill against the lewd misdemeanours of certain of the earl of Cumberland's servants and tenants against my Lord Wharton. [The bill proceeded no further.]

(**32**), vol. I, pp. 5, 6; *Clifford Letters* (**10**), quoted from (**47**), p. 450; the Earl of Cumberland's bill, September 1549, Star Chamber Proceedings 3, 6/46; (**18**), vol. I, p. 519.

document 25
Matters of contention

(a) 1485. Revenue and property rights. Attainders
[A] parliament was held at Westminster, on which so many matters were treated of . . . Among other things, proscriptions, or, as they are more commonly called, 'attainders', were voted against thirty persons; a step which, though bespeaking far greater moderation than was ever witnessed under similar circumstances in the time of King Richard or King Edward, was not taken without considerable

discussion, or, indeed, to speak more truly, considerable censure, of the measures so adopted.

(**28**), p. 511.

(b) 1523. The Commons challenge Wolsey's tax demands and the Lords disavow him

After long reasoning, there were certain [men] appointed to declare the impossibility of this [latest financial] demand to the cardinal, which according to their commission declared to him substantially the poverty and scarceness of the realm. All which reasons and demonstrations he little regarded, and then the said persons most meekly beseeched his grace to move the king's highness to be content with a more easier sum ... [H]e answered that he would rather have his tongue plucked out of his head with a pair of pinsons, than to move the king to take any less sum. With which answer they, almost dismayed, came and made report to the common house, where every day was reasoning but nothing concluded.

Wherefore the cardinal came again to the common house, and desired to be reasoned withal, to whom it was answered that the fashion of the nether house was to hear and not to reason, but among themselves. Then he showed the realm to be of great riches ... After long debating the commons concluded to grant two shillings of the pound ... The grant was reported to the cardinal, which therewith was sore discontent and said that the lords had granted four shillings of the pound, which was proved untrue, for indeed they had granted nothing, but hearkened all upon the commons.

(**12**), fol. cx.

(c) 1515. The Hunne case: laity versus clergy

The temporal lords and justices, at the prompting of those of the said commons house of parliament made instance to the king to maintain his temporal jurisdiction according to his coronation oath ... And then the justices and all the king's counsel, spiritual and temporal, and also certain persons of the said parliament house assembled by command of the king at the said house called Blackfriars in Ludgate on the same matter ... And then, that is, after the justices had heard and fully considered all the reasons and arguments of both parts, that is as well on the part of our said lord the king in maintenance of his temporal jurisdiction as on the part of the clergy in maintenance of their spiritual jurisdiction, they reached the clear decision that all of those of the said convocation [the clergy's assembly]* . . . were in case of praemunire*. And then practically all the lords spiritual and temporal, and many of the knights and others of the commons house of parliament and also all the justices and king's counsel, spiritual and temporal, assembled by command of the king at Baynard's Castle before the king himself to deal with the said cause. At which time the Cardinal Archbishop of York knelt before the king and, for the clergy, said that to his knowledge none of the clergy had ever meant to do anything in derogation of the king's prerogative. And for his own part he said that he owed his whole advancement solely to our lord the king, wherefore he said that he would assent to nothing that would tend to annul or derogate from his royal authority for all the world.

Robert Keilwey's memorandum, (**75**); pp. 149–52.

document 26
1485: Vigorous debate in the House of Commons

The xth day of November there was read a bill for the subsidy between the king and the merchants, which bill was examined amongst us . . . and non conclusion.
The xiiiith day there were arguments . . to non conclusion.
The xxv day of November there were read certain bills, and thereupon were arguments, and nothing passed that day.
The ix day [of December] came in the bill of attaint and sore was questioned with.

(**26**), pp. 186–8.

document 27
Matters of contention: anti-clericalism and religious conflict (see also doc. 25)

(a) 1531. The clerical pardon
The whole clergy of England ever supported and maintained the power legatine of the cardinal, [Wolsey], wherefore the king's council learned said plainly that they all were in the praemunire.* The spiritual lords . . . in their convocation* concluded an humble submission in writing and offered the king one hundred thousand pounds to be their good lord and also to give them a pardon for all offences touching the praemunire by act of parliament . . .

When the parliament was begun . . . the pardon of the spiritual persons was signed with the king's hand and sent to the lords, which in time convenient assented to the bill and sent it to the commons . . . When it was read, divers froward persons would in no wise assent to it, except all men were pardoned, saying that all men which had anything to do with the cardinal were in the same case. The wiser sort answered that they would not compel the king to give them his pardon . . . but they determined first to send the speaker [who] . . . with a convenient number of the common house came to the king's presence and there eloquently declared to the king how the commons sore lamented and bewailed their chance to think or imagine themselves to be out of his gracious favour, because that he had graciously given his pardon of the praemunire to his spiritual subjects and not to them, wherefore they most humbly besought his grace of his accustomed goodness and clemency to include them in the same pardon.

The king wisely answered that he was their Prince and sovereign lord and that they ought not to restrain him of his liberty, nor to compel him to show his mercy, for it was at his pleasure to use the extremity of his laws, or mitigate and pardon the same . . . which pardon he said he might give without their assent, by his great seal . . . and the commons departed very sorrowful and pensive . . .

The king, like a good prince, considered how sorrowful his commons were of the answer that he made them, and thought that they were not quiet, wherefore of his own motion he caused a pardon of the praemunire to be drawn, and signed it with his hand, and sent it to the common house by Christopher Hales his attorney, which bill was soon assented to. Then the commons lovingly thanked the king and much praised his wit, that he had denied it to them when they unworthily demanded it and had bountifully granted it when he perceived that they sorrowed and lamented.

(**12**), fol. clxxxxv.

(b) Bishop Gardiner reminisces about the 1530s

I reasoned once in the parliament house, where was free speech without danger. And there the Lord Audley, then chancellor, to satisfy me familiarly, because I was in some secret estimation, as he then knew – 'Thou art a good fellow, Bishop', quod he (which was the manner of his familiar speech), 'look upon the act of supremacy, and there the king's doings be restrained to spiritual jurisdiction; and in another act it is provided that no spiritual law shall have place contrary to a common law or act of parliament. And [if] this were not,' quod he, 'you bishops would enter in with the king and, by means of his supremacy, order the laity as ye listed. But we will provide,' quod he, 'that the praemunire shall ever hang over your heads, and so we laymen shall be sure to enjoy our inheritance by the common laws and acts of parliament'.

(**21**), p. 392.

document 28

Money matters again

(a) 1529. The King is grateful to Mr Petit
He was xx years burgess for the City of London, and [a freeman] of the grocers' [company], eloquent and well spoken ... King Henry VIII would ask in the parliament time, in his weighty affairs, if Petit were of his side. For once, when the king required to have all those sums of money to be given him by act of parliament, which afore he had borrowed of certain persons, John Petit stood against the bill, saying 'I cannot in my conscience agree and consent that this bill should pass, for I know not my neighbour's estate. They perhaps borrowed it to lend the king. But I know mine own estate, and therefore I freely and frankly give the king that I lent him'.

Reminiscences of John Louthe in (**24**), pp. 25–6.

(b) 1529–36. The Statute of Uses
1532. 14 February. The Imperial Ambassador Chapuys to Emperor Charles V
The King has been trying to obtain in parliament the third part of the feudal property of deceased persons. [He] has hitherto met with a good deal of opposition ... [His] demand has been the occasion of strange words against the King and Council ... [Several] members of the said Parliament have made use in public of very strong language against [him].

(**2**), vol. V, no. 805.

1532. The King meets a deputation of Commons' members
'[M]ethinketh that you should not contend with me that I am your sovereign lord and king, considering that I seek peace and quietness

of you; for I have sent to you a bill concerning wards and primer seisin in the which things I am greatly wronged; wherefore I have offered you reason, as I think, yea, and so thinketh all the Lords . . .; therefore I assure you, if you will not take some reasonable end now when it is offered, I will search out the extremity of the law and then will I not offer you so much again'. With this answer the Speaker and his company departed.

(**12**), p. 785.

1553. Settlement of the lands of Lord Dacre of the South
The yearly value of his lands is £1,042–17s–1d.

Deductions for fees and annuities £100, and lady Fenys' jointure, £110–14s–10d. Total value at his death, £832–3s–3d.

Further deductions: the manors of Burgham and Nassheall, willed to John Fenys, one of his younger sons, the manor of Horsford and all his lands in Norfolk, willed to Thos. Fenys, another of his younger sons, and the manor of Cowham, appointed by his feoffees for lady Fenys' jointure, £121–3s–7d. Residue, £711.

Further deductions: The manor of Wrentham and all the lands in Suffolk, the manors of Ewhurst, Bukholt, South Berwyke, Dolhams, Knyghtes, and Peny Landez, Sussex, the manor of Compton Mounceux, Hampshire, assigned for the performance of his will £214–12s–8d. The residue, which the executors should have till the heir comes to the age of 24 years, whereof there is 500 mks willed to Anne Fenys, lord Dacre's niece, £497–0s–4d.

The manor of Hurstmonceux for one year after his decease is for the finding of the household there.

(**2**), vol. VI, no. 1590.

1535. The judges' opinion on the Dacre settlement
The validity of [wills] was argued by all but two of the judges in Exchequer Chamber in Trinity term, 1535. They debated the matter in the presence of the lord chancellor [Thomas Audley] and the king's secretary [Thomas Cromwell].

The chancellor, the secretary, and three judges were of the opinion 'that such a will was of no effect but void, for no land is devisable by will . . . [Secondly] the land was in the feoffees [the trustees] for all purposes and it is contrary to reason that *cestui que use* [the beneficiary], who in effect has nothing, should make a will and by this give the land to another, to whoever he pleases'.

Spilman [Justice of the Court of King's Bench], Shelley and Fitzherbert [Justice of the Court of Common Pleas] and Fitzjames [Chief Justice of the Court of King's Bench] are of the contrary opinion, that such a will is a declaration of the trust . . . and the feoffee is obliged in conscience to perform this . . . And he [the devisor of the will] gives nothing in the land by his will, but only his use, and the [legal] estate of the feoffee is not impaired in any way by this . . . And Port [Justice of the Court of King's Bench] is of the same opinion. But he spoke so low that the said chancellor and secretary understood him to be of the contrary opinion. And because of this they thought that the greater number of the justices were of opinion with them. And therefore all the justices were commanded to appear before the king. And he ordered them to assemble to again an opinion. And those who were of opinion that the will was void should have of the king *bon thanke*. And then the justices reassembled before the said chancellor and secretary and debated this question, and Fitzjames, Fitzherbert and Spilman came round to the opinion of the chancellor, secretary and the other justices, who were men of great reason and the number of them was greater, and they conformed themselves to their opinion. But Shelley was not there because he was ill . . .

(**116**), pp. 8–9.

1536. Robert Aske on the Statute of Uses
[Aske was one of the leaders of the Northern Rebellion in 1536] It would be profitable for worshipful men, having lands, that the said statute should be annulled or qualified, so that they might declare their will of parcel of their lands for payment of their debts and marriage of their children . . . Also great men cannot have such credit with merchants or so much money to do the king's service when needful . . . because most men's lands are entailed [i.e. they had to descend to the heir and could not be bequeathed to anyone else].

(**2**), vol. XII, pt 1, no. 901, pp. 406–7.

(c) 1553. The Duke of Northumberland is nervous about the Commons
I am of the opinion that we need not to be so ceremonious as to imagine the object[ion]s of every froward person, but rather to burden their minds and hearts with the king's majesty's extreme debts and necessity grown and risen by such orations and motions as can-

not be denied by no man, and that we need not to seem to make account to the commons of his majesty's liberality and bountifulness in augmenting or advancing of his nobles, or of his benevolence showed to any his servants, lest you might thereby make them wanton and give them occasion to take hold of your own arguments ...

Northumberland to William Cecil, 14 January 1553, **(27)**, 10/18/fol. 6

document

1553. Bishop Gardiner resists Mary I's choice of a foreign husband

17 November. Renard to the Emperor

Sire: The queen of England told me yesterday that the speaker of parliament, accompanied by the duke of Norfolk, the earls of Arundel, Shrewsbury, Derby and Pembroke, the bishops of Durham, Winchester and Norwich, [the] lords privy seal and Paget, and several other noblemen, councillors, and members of the lower house, came to her and held, on behalf of parliament, a long and carefully composed discourse, full of art and rhetoric and illustrated by historic examples, in order to arrive at two objects: to induce her to marry, and to choose a husband in England ... [The queen replied that] parliament was not accustomed to use such language to the kings of England, nor was it suitable or respectful that it should do so ... She called the members of the nobility to witness whether they had ever seen such doings, and whether it was right to utter such words ... [W]hen the members of parliament had retired and a few councillors, among them the bishop of Winchester, remained, the earl of Arundel told the bishop that he had lost his post of chancellor that day, for the queen had usurped it [it was customary for the monarch to reply through the Chancellor], and laughed at him. And the queen told me plainly that she had soon understood Winchester's wiles and appraised his leanings ...

20 November. Renard to the Emperor

In the course of conversation [Winchester] also mentioned the marriage question, whereat the queen, seeing that he raised it of his own accord, told the bishop that she had suspected him of having inspired the speaker [of the commons], because he had already used to her all the speaker's arguments in favour of Courtenay ... The chancellor replied with tears that he had never instructed the speaker, either by word of mouth or in writing, but confessed that he had mentioned those considerations to him, and that it was true he had been fond of Courtenay since they were in prison together. In reply the queen asked him whether it would be suitable to force her to marry a man, because the bishop had conceived a friendship for him in prison . . .

(**1**), vol. XI, pp. 363–5, 372.

document 30
'Winchester's faction'

1547.27 October. Bishop Gardiner of Winchester writes to Protector Somerset from the Fleet Prison
If your Grace should now any ways comfort me in prison with the least token of gentleness, you might be noted to favour Winchester's faction, as some term it; whereas, I take God to record, I never joined myself with any man, nor have secretly encouraged any man to be of my opinion.
[Probably after 20] November 1547. Another letter from Gardiner to Somerset
If it should be of any man through policy to keep me from the parliament, it were good to be remembered whether mine absence from the upper house, with the absence of those I have used to name in the nether house, will not engender more cause of objection, if opportunity serve hereafter, than my presence with such as I should appoint were there . . .

(**21**), pp. 405, 424.

document 31
1554. Delinquent peers

19(?) April. Lord Paget to Renard
For the love of God, Sir, persuade the queen to dissolve parliament at once and send off to the provinces the men who have been appointed to govern them. The weather is beginning to be warm, and men's tempers will wax warm too; and I see that this man's [Bishop Gardiner] private leanings will cause him to bring forward proposals that will heat the people altogether too much . . .

22 April. Renard to the Emperor
Sire: Since I last wrote, quarrels, jealousy and ill-will have increased among the councillors . . . What one does, another undoes; that one

advises, another opposes . . . Paget and his party have openly combined in parliament to fight certain bills on religion, introduced without their knowledge and providing for the punishment of heretics . . . And whereas a bill was brought before parliament to make it high treason to plot against his highness's [Prince Philip] life when in England or take up arms against him, the lords have refused to pass the second clause, making it a treasonable offence to take up arms against his highness.

1 and 6 May. Renard to the Emperor
The queen holds Paget in grave suspicion because of two actions of his, which she explained to me. The first was when it was proposed in parliament to proclaim guilty of rebellion those who should take up arms against his highness; for Paget opposed the measure more stubbornly than any one else . . . The second was that, when penalties against the heretics were being discussed, he incited the lords not to consent . . . [Paget] induced several of the lords to oppose the measure, persuading them that it was being introduced in order to deprive them of the Church property now in their hands . . . He gave no thought to the queen's reputation, the quiet of her realm or his highness's coming, but allowed himself to be led by his hatred of the chancellor . . .

(**1**), vol. XII, pp. 220–1, 230, 238.

Parliamentary sessions, 1485–1558

Parliament		Date of sessions	Dissolution dates
Henry VII			
1485–86	(1)	7 November–10 December 1485	
	(2)	23 January–c.4 March 1486	c.4 March 1486
1487		9 November–December 1487	December 1487
1489–90	(1)	13 January–23 February 1489	
	(2)	25 January–27 February 1490	27 February 1490
1491–92	(1)	17 October–4 November 1491	
	(2)	26 January–5 March 1492	5 March 1492
1495		14 October–21/22 December 1495	21/22 December 1495
1497		16 January–13 March 1497	13 March 1497
1504		25 January–(?) April 1504	April 1504
Henry VIII			
1510		21 January–23 February 1510	23 February 1510
1512–14	(1)	4 February–30 March 1512	
	(2)	4 November–20 December 1512	
	(3)	23 January–4 March 1514	4 March 1514
1515	(1)	5 February–5 April 1515	
	(2)	12 November–22 December 1515	22 December 1515
1523	(1)	15 April–21 May 1523	
	(2)	10 June–13 August 1523	13 August 1523
1529–36	(1)	3 November–17 December 1529	
	(2)	16 January–31 March 1531	
	(3)	15 January–14 May 1532	
	(4)	4 February–7 April 1533	
	(5)	15 January–30 March 1534	
	(6)	3 November–18 December 1534	
	(7)	4 February–14 April 1536	14 April 1536

1536		8 June–18 July	18 July 1536
1539–40	(1)	28 April–28 June 1539	
	(2)	12 April–24 July 1540	24 July 1540
1542–44	(1)	16 January–1 April	
	(2)	22 January–12 May 1543	
	(3)	14 January–29 March 1544	29 March 1544
1545–47	(1)	23 November–24 December 1545	
	(2)	14–31 January 1547	Automatically dissolved by Henry VIII's death

Edward VI

1547–52	(1)	4 November–24 December 1547	
	(2)	24 November 1548–14 March 1549	
	(3)	4 November 1549–1 February 1550	
	(4)	23 January–15 April 1552	15 April 1552
1553		1–31 March 1553	31 March 1553

Mary I

1553		5 October–6 December 1553	6 December 1553
1554		2 April–5 May 1554	5 May 1554
1554/5		12 November 1554–16 January 1555	16 January 1555
1555		21 October–9 December 1555	9 December 1555
1558	(1)	20 January–7 March 1558	
	(2)	5–17 November 1558	Automatically dissolved by Mary I's death

Glossary

John Calvin   John Calvin stressed the omnipotence of God, who had predestined some (the elect) to be saved and others (the reprobate) to be damned. His practical importance derived (1) from his theology set forth in his *Institutes of the Christian Religion*; (2) the consequent growth of an international Calvinist movement; (3) his obsessive drive to erect God's kingdom on earth–which he attempted to achieve in Geneva.

Convocation   The provincial assemblies of the clergy. The province of Canterbury covered southern and central England, and Wales; the province of York had its own convocation for the clergy of northern England.

Douceurs   The term encompassed everything from legitimate favours, gifts and gratuities for services, to blatant bribes.

Fee'd   A professional man, usually a lawyer, was 'fee'd' when he received a retainer: a regular payment which entitled the payer to call upon his services when they were required.

Feudal aids   Henry VII sought feudal aids in 1504 for the knighting of his heir Arthur (who, however, had been knighted years before and was now dead) and for the marriage of his eldest daughter Margaret. They could not be levied without the assent of those who held their property on feudal tenure – or at least of their representatives in Parliament. In contrast, feudal *dues* (*incidents*) required no such approval. They were often burdensome, and consequently landowners attempted to conceal their obligations whenever possible. But, especially in the later years of his reign, Henry worked energetically to uncover them. Feudal aids could be collected only after a national investigation to discover the property held by feudal tenure. This accounts for the Commons' concern in 1504.

Field of the Cloth of Gold, 1520   The occasion, ostensibly a diplomatic *rapprochement* between Henry VIII and Francis I of France, was little more than a hollow and very costly extravaganza of lavish pageantry, jousting and entertainment–a competitive exercise in which the two kings and their courts attempted to outdo each other.

Fifteenths and tenths   The most important source of parliamentary revenue between 1300 and 1500 was a property tax: 10 per cent on crown lands and urban communities, and a levy of one-fifteenth in the rest of the kingdom. From 1334 it became a fixed sum, to which each district contributed a specified amount.

Livery   As the king was the chief feudal overlord in the realm, many landowners owed feudal obligations to him: in particular, if one of them died whilst his heir was a minor, the latter became a ward of the crown. When the royal ward's minority ended, he had to pay a livery–an 'entry' fine–when he assumed personal control of his estates.

Martin Luther   The protest of Luther, an Augustinian friar, against what he regarded as a corrupt Church, papacy and doctrine sparked a religious Reformation. Much of Germany, especially in the north, responded to his protest and became Protestant, rejecting both the Pope and Catholic doctrine. The Lutheran movement then spread north (into Scandinavia), east into Hungary, and westwards along the trade routes, even into England.

Praemunire   In the late fourteenth century, praemunire was a specific offence, namely encroachment by ecclesiastical jurisdiction on the competence of the King's courts. By the 1530s it had become more vague, wide-reaching, and dangerous: any invasion of the King's 'regality' was a praemunire offence, punishable by loss of goods and indefinite imprisonment.

Prebendary   A canon (member) of a cathedral chapter in receipt of a stipend (a financial allowance).

Sign manual   The monarch's signature.

Strode's case   When Richard Strode promoted a parliamentary bill harmful to the tin-mining interest in the West Country, he was punished by the stannary courts. These were special tribunals whose function was to protect the tin industry. An Act of Henry VIII not only indemnified Strode but–more important–stated that anything said or done in the high court of Parliament could not be punished in the lesser courts of the realm.

Sumptuary laws   Sumptuary legislation was a technique of social control. The purpose was to identify everyone's position in the social hierarchy by regulating, in very precise terms, the materials which each rank could wear.

Three fifteenths   A property tax (see *fifteenths and tenths* above), in this case amounting to three fifteenths or 20 per cent of the value of the property.

Treason laws   Treason was essentially an offence against the person of the monarch or members of the royal family, in particular conspiring to kill, raising rebellion or levying war. In the sixteenth century, however, the treasons enumerated in the Act of 1352 were enlarged to catch those who denied the validity of Henry VIII's marriages, the royal succession or the royal supremacy over the Church.

Bibliography

DOCUMENTS AND CONTEMPORARY ACCOUNTS

1   Bergenroth, G. A., Hume, M. A. S., and Tyler, R. (eds), *Calendar of State Papers Spanish*, 13 vols, London, 1862–1954.

2   Brewer, J. S., Gairdner, J., Brodie, R. M. (eds), *Letters and Papers, Foreign and Domestic, of the Reign of Henry VIII*, London, 1862–1932.

3   Bond, M. F. (ed.), *The Manuscripts of the House of Lords*, new series, Addenda, London, 1514–1714, 1962.

4   Brown, R., Bentinck, C. *et al.* (eds), *Calendar of State Papers and Manuscripts, Relating to English Affairs, existing in the Archives and Collections of Venice*, 9 vols, London, 1864–98.

5   Cobbet, W., Howell, T. B. *et al.* (eds), *A Complete Collection of State Trials*, 42 vols, London, 1816–98.

6   Coke, E., *Institutes of the Laws of England*, 4 pts, London 1628–44.

7   Corporation of London Record Office. Repertories of the Court of Aldermen.

8   Dasent, J. R. (ed.), *Acts of the Privy Council*, 32 vols, London, 1890–1907.

9   D'Ewes, Sir Simonds, *The Journals of all the Parliaments during the Reign of Queen Elizabeth, both of the House of Lords and House of Commons*, London, 1682.

10 Dickens, A. G. (ed.), *Clifford Letters of the Sixteenth Century*, Surtees Society, 172, Durham, 1962.

11 Foxe, John, *Acts and Monuments*, ed. J. Pratt, 8 vols, London, 1870.

12 Halle, Edward, *The Union of the Two Noble and Illustre Famelies of Lancastre and York*, London, 1550, reprinted Menston, 1970.

13 Haynes, S. and Murdin, W. (eds), *Collection of State Papers. . . left by William Cecil, Lord Burghley*, 2 vols, London, 1740–59.

14 *Historical Manuscripts Commission Reports: City of Exeter*, 73, 1916.

15 *Historical Manuscripts Commission: Marquess of Salisbury (Hatfield Mss)*, Part I, 1883.

Bibliography

16 Holinshed, R., *Chronicles of England, Scotland, and Ireland*, ed. H. Ellis, London, 1807–8.

17 Jordan, W. K. (ed.), *The Chronicle and Political Papers of King Edward VI*, Allen and Unwin, 1966.

18 *Journals of the House of Lords*, vols I, II, London, 1846.

19 Luders, A., Tomlins, T. E., Raithby, J. *et al.* (eds), *Statutes of the Realm*, 11 vols, I–IV, London, 1810–28.

20 Merriman, R. B., *Life and Letters of Thomas Cromwell*, 2 vols, Clarendon Press, 1902.

21 Muller, J. A. (ed.), *The Letters of Stephen Gardiner*, Cambridge University Press, 1933.

22 Nichols, J. G. (ed.), *The Chronicle of Calais in the Reigns of Henry VII, and Henry VIII to the year 1540*, Camden Society, 35, 1846.

23 Nichols, J. G. (ed.), *Chronicle of the Grey Friars of London*, Camden Society, 53, 1852.

24 Nichols, J. G. (ed.), *Narratives of the Days of the Reformation*, Camden Society, old series 77, 1859.

25 Noailles, Messieurs de, *Ambassades en Angleterre*, ed. Vertot d'Aubeuf, R. A. and Villaret, C., 5 vols, Leyden, 1763.

26 Pronay, N. and Taylor, J. (eds), *Parliamentary Texts of the Later Middle Ages*, Clarendon Press, 1980.

27 Public Record Office, State Papers Domestic.

28 Riley, H. T. (ed.), *Ingulph's Chronicle of the Abbey of Croyland*, London, 1854.

29 St German, Christopher, *A Dialogue betwixt a Doctor of Divinity and a Student in the Laws of England*, London, 1530.

30 Scobell, H., *Remembrances of some Methods, Orders and Proceedings heretofore used and observed in the House of Lords*, London, 1657.

31 Sylvester, R. S. and Harding, D. P. (eds) *Two Early Tudor Lives*, Yale University Press, 1973.

32 Vardon, T. and May, T. E. (eds), *Journals of the House of Commons*, vol.I (1547–1628), London, 1803.

33 Ward, P. L. (ed.), *William Lambarde's Notes on the Procedures and Privileges of the House of Commons (1584)*, Her Majesty's Stationery Office, 1977.

THE MEDIEVAL BACKGROUND

34 Chrimes, S. B., *Lancastrians, Yorkists and Henry VII*, Macmillan, 1964.

35 Lander, J..R., *Conflict and Stability in Fifteenth-Century England*, Hutchinson, 1969.

36 Lander, J. R., *Crown and Nobility, 1450–1509*, Edward Arnold, 1976.

37 Lander, J. R., *Government and Community. England 1450–1509*, Edward Arnold, 1980.

38 Lockyer, R., *Henry VII*, Longman (Seminar Studies in History), 1968.

39 McFarlane, K. B., *The Nobility of Later Medieval England*, Clarendon Press, 1973.

40 McKisack, M., *The Parliamentary Representation of the English Boroughs during the Middle Ages*, Oxford University Press., 1962.

41 Roskell, J. S., *The Commons in the Parliament of 1422. English Society and Parliamentary Representation under the Lancastrians*, Manchester University Press, 1954.

42 Roskell, J. S., 'The Problem of the Attendance of the Lords in Medieval Parliaments', *Bulletin of the Institute of Historical Research*, 29, 1956.

43 Roskell, J. S., *The Commons and their Speakers in English Parliaments, 1376–1523*, Manchester University Press, 1965.

44 Wilkinson, B., *Constitutional History of England in the Fifteenth Century, 1399–1485*, Longman, 1964.

45 Wilkinson, B., *The Later Middle Ages in England, 1216–1485*, Longman, 1969.

EARLY TUDOR PARLIAMENTS

Books

46 Bernard, G. W., *War, Taxation and Rebellion in Early Tudor England: Henry VIII, Wolsey and the Amicable Grant of 1525*, Harvester Press, 1986.

47 Bindoff, S. T. (ed.), *The House of Commons, 1509–1558*, 3 vols, Secker and Warburg, 1982.

48 Bush, M. L., *The Government Policy of Proctector Somerset*, Edward Arnold, 1976.

49 Chrimes, S. B., *Henry VII*, Eyre Methuen, 1972.

50 Cokayne, G. E. (ed.), *The Complete Peerage of England, Scotland, Ireland, Great Britain, and the United Kingdom extant, extinct, or dormant*, ed. V. Gibbs, 13 vols in 14, London, 1910–59.

51 Coleman, C. and Starkey, D. (eds), *Revolution Reassessed: Revisions in the History of Tudor Government and Administration*, Clarendon Press, Oxford, 1986.

52   Elton, G. R., *The Tudor Revolution in Government: Administrative Changes in the Reign of Henry VIII*, Cambridge University Press, 1953.

53   Elton, G. R., *England under the Tudors*, Methuen, 2nd edition, 1974.

54   Elton, G. R., *Reform and Renewal: Thomas Cromwell and the Commonweal*, Cambridge University Press, 1973.

55   Elton, G. R., *Reform and Reformation: England 1509–1558*, Edward Arnold, 1977.

56   Elton, G. R., *The Tudor Constitution: Documents and Commentary*, Cambridge University Press, 2nd edn, 1982.

57   Fox, A., *Thomas More: History and Providence*, Blackwell, 1982.

58   Fox, A. and Guy, J., *Reassessing the Henrician Age: Humanism, Politics and Reform, 1500–1550*, Blackwell, 1986.

59   Gasquet, F. A. and Bishop, E., *Edward VI and the Book of Common Prayer*, London, 1890.

60   Graves, M. A. R., *The House of Lords in the Parliaments of Edward VI and Mary*, Cambridge University Press, 1981.

61   Graves, M. A. R., *The Tudor Parliaments: Crown, Lords and Commons, 1485–1603*, Longman (Studies in Modern History Series), 1985.

62   Graves, M. A. R., *Elizabethan Parliaments, 1559–1601*, Longman (Seminar Studies in History) 1987.

63   Guy, J. A., *The Public Career of Sir Thomas More*, Harvester Press, 1980.

64   Guy, John, *Tudor England*, Oxford University Press, 1988

65   Hoak, D., *The King's Council in the Reign of Edward VI*, Cambridge, 1976.

66   Jordan, W. K., *Edward VI: The Young King. The Protectorship of the Duke of Somerset*, Allen and Unwin, 1968

67   Jordan, W. K., *Edward VI: The Threshold of Power. The Dominance of the Duke of Northumberland*, Allen and Unwin, 1970.

68   Lehmberg, S. E., *The Reformation Parliament, 1529–1536*, Cambridge University Press, 1970.

69   Lehmberg, S. E., *The Later Parliaments of Henry VIII, 1536–1547*, Cambridge University Press, 1977.

70   Loach, J., *Parliament and the Crown in the Reign of Mary Tudor*, Clarendon Press, Oxford, 1986.

71   Loades, D. M., *The Reign of Mary Tudor: Politics, government and religion in England, 1553–1558*, Ernest Benn, 1979.

72   Miller, H. *Henry VIII and the English Nobility*, Blackwell, 1986.

73 Neale, J. E., *The Elizabethan House of Commons*, Cape, 1949.
74 Neale, J. E., *Elizabeth I and her Parliaments*, 2 vols, Cape, 1953, 1957.
75 Ogle, A., *The Tragedy of the Lollards Tower*, Oxford, 1949.
76 Pollard, A. F., *England under the Protector Somerset*, Russell and Russell, 1900.
77 Pollard, A.F., *The Evolution of Parliament*, Longman, 2nd ed., 1964.
78 Powell, J. E. and Wallis, K., *The House of Lords in the Middle Ages*, Weidenfeld and Nicolson, 1968.
79 Scarisbrick, J. J., *Henry VIII*, Eyre and Spottiswoode, 1968.
80 Storey, R. L., *The Reign of Henry VII*, Blandford, 1968.
81 Strype, J., *Ecclesiastical Memorials*, 3 vols, Oxford, 1822.
82 Sturge, C., *Cuthbert Tunstal*, London, 1938.
83 Tytler, P. F. (ed.), *England under the reigns of Edward VI and Mary*, 2 vols, London, 1839.
84 Williams, P., *The Tudor Regime*, Clarendon Press, 1979.

Articles, essays and pamphlets

The following abbreviations are used:

B.I.H.R.	*Bulletin of the Institute of Historical Research*
B.J.R.L.	*Bulletin of the John Rylands Library*
E.H.R.	*English Historical Review*
H.J.	*Historical Journal*
Parl. Hist.	*Parliamentary History*
P & P	*Past and Present*
T.R.H.S.	*Transactions of the Royal Historical Society*

85 Alsop, J. D., 'The Theory and Practice of Tudor Taxation', *E.H.R*, 97, 1982.
86 Alsop, J. D., 'Innovation in Tudor Taxation', *E.H.R*, 99, 1984.
87 Collinson, P., 'Puritans, Men of Business and Elizabethan Parliaments', *Parliamentary History*, 7, part 2, pp. 187–211, 1988.
88 Cooper, J. P., 'Henry VII's Last Years Reconsidered', *H.J.*, 2, no. 2, pp. 103–29, 1959.
89 Elton, G. R., 'Rapacity and remorse', *H.J.*, 1, no. 1, pp. 21–39, 1958.
90 Elton, G. R., 'Henry VII: A Restatement', *H.J.*, 4, no. 1, pp. 1–29, 1961.

91   Elton, G. R., 'King or Minister? The Man behind the Henrician Reformation', *History*, new series, 39, pp. 216–32, 1954.

92   Elton, G. R., 'The Tudor Revolution: A Reply', *P & P*, 29, pp. 26–49, 1964.

93   Elton, G. R., 'A Revolution in Tudor History?', *P & P*, 32, pp. 103–9, 1965.

94   Elton, G. R., 'The Early Journals of the House of Lords', *E.H.R.*, 89, pp. 481–512, 1974.

95   Elton, G. R., 'Tudor Government: The Points of Contact. I. Parliament', *T.R.H.S.*, 5th Series, 24, pp. 183–200, 1974.

96   Elton, G. R., 'Studying the History of Parliament' in *Studies in Tudor and Stuart Politics and Government: Papers and Reviews, 1946–1972*, vol. 2, pp. 3–18, Cambridge University Press, 1974.

97   Elton, G. R., ' "The Body of the Whole Realm": Parliament and Representation in Medieval and Tudor England' in *Studies in Tudor and Stuart Politics and Government: Papers and Reviews, 1946–1972*, vol. 2, pp. 19–61, Cambridge University Press, 1974.

98   Elton, G. R., 'Taxation for War and Peace in Early-Tudor England', in *War and Economic Developments: Essays in Memory of David Joslin*, ed. J. M. Winter, pp. 33–48, Cambridge University Press, 1975.

99   Elton, G. R., 'The Sessional Printing of Statutes, 1484 to 1547', in Ives, E. W., Knecht, R. J. and Scarisbrick, J.J. (eds), *Wealth and Power in Tudor England*, pp. 68–86, Athlone Press, 1978.

100 Elton, G.R., 'The Rolls of Parliament, 1449–1547', *H.J.*, xxii, pp. 1–29, 1979.

101 Elton, G. R., 'Enacting Clauses and Legislative Initiative, 1559–81', *B.I.H.R*, liii, pp. 183–91, 1980.

102 Graves, M.A.R., 'The House of Lords and the Politics of Opposition, April-May 1554' in Wood, G. A. and O'Connor, P. S. (eds), *W. P. Morrill: A Tribute*, pp. 1–20, Otago University Press, 1973.

103 Graves, M. A. R., 'The Mid-Tudor House of Lords: Forgotten Member of the Parliamentary Trinity' in McGregor, F. and Wright, N. (eds), *European History and its Historians*, pp. 23–31, Adelaide University Press, 1977.

104 Harriss, G. L. and Williams, Penry, 'A Revolution in Tudor History?', *P & P*, 25, pp. 3–58, 1963.

105   Harriss, G. L. and Williams, Penry, 'A Revolution in Tudor History?', *P & P*, 31, pp. 87–96, 1965.

106   Harriss, G. L., 'Theory and Practice in Royal Taxation: Some Observations', *E.H.R*, 97, 1982.

107   Ives, E. W., 'The Genesis of the Statute of Uses', *E.H.R.*, 82, pp. 673–97, 1967.

108   Loach, J., 'Conservatism and Consent in Parliament, 1547–59' in *The Mid-Tudor Polity, c.1540–1560*, J. Loach and R. Tittler (eds), pp. 9–28, Macmillan, 1980.

109   Loach, J., 'Parliament: A New Air?' in C. Coleman and D. Starkey (eds), *Revolution Reassessed: Revisions in the History of Tudor Government and Administration*, Clarendon Press, Oxford, 1986.

110   Miller, H., 'London and Parliament in the Reign of Henry VIII', *B.I.H.R.*, 35, pp. 128–49, 1962.

111   Miller, H., 'Attendance in the House of Lords during the reign of Henry VIII', *H.J.*, 10, 4, pp. 325–51, 1967.

112   Miller, H., 'Lords and Commons: relations between the two Houses of Parliament, 1509–1558', *Parl.Hist.*, I, pp. 13–24, 1982.

113   Notestein, W., 'The Winning of the Initiative by the House of Commons', *Proceedings of the British Academy*, xi, 1924.

114   Roskell, J. S., 'Perspectives in English Parliamentary History', *B. J. R. L.*, xlvi, pp. 448–75, 1964.

115   Schofield, Roger, 'Taxation and the Political Limits of the Tudor State' in Claire Cross, David Loades and J. J. Scarisbrick (eds), *Law and Government under the Tudors*, Cambridge University Press, 1988.

116   Simpson, A. B., 'The Equitable Doctrine of Consideration and the Law of Uses', *University of Toronto Law Journal*, 16, 1965.

117   Wolffe, B. P., *Yorkist and Early Tudor Government, 1461–1509*, Historical Association (Aids for Teachers Series no. 12), 1966.

Index